Endo

"Every day has the potential to become a better day in anyone's life. The key is to remember God's promises and God's provision. Charese Sailor has written a wonderful devotional that walks us daily into the wonderful promises of God. As this devotional builds your faith, you will find your life soaring into new dimensions you always longed for!"

TIM STOREY
Celebrity Life Coach

"So, you want to be a warrior, start overcoming, and walk in your destined purpose? This is the biblical encouragement and wisdom you need. Charese is a true warrior and an overcomer in her own life, but it doesn't happen overnight. Every single reflection is sure to speak to your soul. Now, you have a powerful tool along with your Bible to cheer you on every step of the way."

FANCHON STINGER
Emmy Award-Winning News Anchor

"Go Get Your Life" is like a fire hydrant of gushing inspiration. Charese Sailor weaves life experiences with Biblical teaching in a way that makes this a must-read every day as one starts their day. It connects, it's real, it helps us both blossom and bloom."

PAUL LAMBERT
Award-Winning Broadway Producer

"The combination of Charese Sailor and Go Get Your Life are two must-haves in your life journey. Charese is not only a seer who will get you all the way together, honey, but she's also a compassionate soul whose words uplift and inspire anyone who reads or hears her voice. From the moment I met Charese, I could feel God moving and speaking through her. Our words are powerful, and Charese's are mighty!"

CANDICE VERNON
Award-Winning Executive Producer & Director

"Go Get Your Life! It is a Spiritual Guide to unlocking, healing, and overcoming those things that no longer serve you or your purpose. I suggest you Go Get Your Life with Coach Charese today!"

BRANDON BLACKWELL
Audio Engineer For Various Award-Winning Artists

"If you thought it was too late to attain the life you desire, you are highly mistaken. Just as the title suggests, "Go Get Your Life" is inspiring and reminds you that it is never too late to go after everything God has for you. I enjoyed how Charese Sailor uses life lessons to illustrate and remind us that we all struggle at times. " Go Get Your Life" acknowledges our struggles, and provides us with biblical reminders that during our challenges and in our weakness, God is strong, and as long as we do not give up, we can get the life we desire."

SONYA WEAVER
Founder & CEO of Deals With B.O.B.

Testimonials

This book is a very simple guide to follow with easy action steps that don't make me feel overwhelmed. I've accomplished a task each day! I have discovered some hard truths about myself that I need to improve. Whew, this book is helping me take the necessary steps I need to go get my life!

Shawn D, MI

Reading over my notes from Day One of <u>Go Get Your Life!</u> and there are so many golden nuggets in that text alone! This book is going to bless everyone who reads it!

Mekylla S, MI

Charese is an extraordinary woman who speaks from the heart and channels the divine. She has encouraged me to be the best version of myself and has inspired and guided me to become even more successful than I could have ever imagined. She's like my personal guardian angel on earth and every time we speak I am not only blessed but enriched. I would encourage anyone who has an opportunity to work with her (through coaching or reading her book) to do so immediately. She will change your life!

Jeremy D, CA

An ANOINTED COACH! I've had many come along and inspire, but COACH CHARESE IS THE REAL DEAL! To receive business mentoring AND A WORD FROM HEAVEN IS A DOUBLE BLESSING! Thank you for allowing God to use you!

TB, MI

I finished my clarity call this week, and it exceeded my expectations. My first call with Coach Charese has already armed me with the tools I need to begin breaking through the challenges prohibiting me from focusing on my goals. Charese, I cannot thank you enough for your passion, focus, and dedication! This is going to be an amazing journey. I am so excited to see my life through a different lens.

Caroline C, MI

This was a great experience! It helped shed light on my weak areas in reference to completing tasks, and helped me to get focused and structured in doing the things that I knew needed to be completed. I set some pretty tough goals for myself, (there were three), and one I completed 15 days early, and the other I see manifesting daily!! I'm thankful to Coach Charese, for her commitment to bringing out and pulling out the best in her fellow Human Beings!!

Sheryl B, GA

My experience with Charese Sailor and the "F" Your Life Up challenge group has been nothing less than phenomenal! Like many of us, I had a lot of moving parts in my life and was hesitant to embark upon another added component. However, thanks be to God that I was obedient to allow myself to be stretched to reach my personal business goals.

Before being coached by Charese, the THOUGHT of where I wanted my businesses to go was vividly in my mind. Charese used practical analogies, prophetic words, and real-life examples to get me to WRITE MY VISION and make it plain! Like a parent does with a child not quite ready to be independent, she encouraged me, held my hand, AND HELD ME ACCOUNTABLE! I now can see the runway and have landed my craft! Thank God for Charese, her passion and her gifts to make this opportunity possible!

Tricia B, MI

Go Get Your Life! is an effective approach to spiritually grounded personal coaching aligned with overall health and wellness awareness…a perfect blend put together by a true Coach.

Marcus S, MI

My clarity call with Coach Charese has me feeling like Michael Jackson, "Girl, you rocked my world"!

Believe it when I say, help was just a call away. Coach Charese Sailor straightened me out on the first call with several love taps. In a matter of 20 minutes, my clouds were clear & I could see a ray of sunshine in the sky. It felt so good to arrive at the "airport for my life" & receive my "boarding pass" to access what I desire for my life!

Erica R, MI

A clear vision and a solid plan are so important when you're committed to changing your life. Thank you Coach Charese for helping me to "write the vision and make it plain". The next 40 days will be EPIC!!!

Lisa G, GA

I had the wonderful opportunity to have a clarity call with Coach Charese. It was awesome. In just that short time, she crafted solutions to make my life run flawlessly. We cannot always see for ourselves holes and spaces in how we use our time, or areas that may devalue or devour our life. Humbling yourself for someone to pick out the bumps has made all the difference. Although you are great, to be greater some things need to get lined up. Coach Charese was able to help me do just that! Thank you Coach Charese!

Sonia G, MI

I was having an off day and I had a scheduled clarity call with Coach Charese. Honestly, I was going to cancel it. I'm so glad I didn't! After our call I felt better, and I'm now ready to go get my life and all God has for me. Thank you!

Pam S, MI

Thank you, Charese, for my clarity call session. I am grateful for the opportunity to have had a conversation with you about the dreams that have been in my spirit. I know that you will walk by my side and hold me accountable. I walked away today with one action item and two concepts to meditate on for the next steps. I am committed to doing the work to realize my full purpose and walk in the greatness that God has for my life. Thanks for being with me on this journey, my friend, my sister. I love you. Thanks for sharing your gifts with me!

Jamie D, GA

I'm so thankful and full of love and appreciation for Coach Charese. My clarity call session has initiated a fire and realignment to my purpose and goals. I literally experienced a shift in my thinking and it has caused an immediate activation!!

After work yesterday...I got into my workspace and completed all of my vision board goals!! My husband had to eventually tell me .."Go to bed" lol...Thank you, Coach Charese thank you!!! for allowing your gifts to flow!! My limiting beliefs are canceled!! Moving forward in 2021 with power!!

Patricia S. MI

Thank God for my sister Charese and her many, many gifts... but this one has really blessed me! I have gotten more done in the past two days than I have in two months. I've been trying to work on my projects since the beginning of the quarantine and just was not able to put my hands on them consistently. With the proper coach and accountability partner in Charese Sailor, I am able to see my projects being birthed! She definitely does have a gift for this, and she's always been a leader and encourager, but I am thanking her from the bottom of my heart for a "Clarity Call" where she gave me specific instructions tailor-made to coach me into making my dreams and visions come true! Where God is taking her, she might not always be so easily accessible. Therefore, I suggest you "F" your life up with Coach Charese now...and GO GET YOUR LIFE... because I am!

Georgie S, MI

28 27 26 25 24 23   9 8 7 6 5 4 3 2 1

GO GET YOUR LIFE!

Copyright ©2023 Charese D. Sailor

All rights reserved. Except as permitted under the U.S. Copyright Act of 1976, no part of this publication may be reproduced, distributed, or transmitted in any form by any means, or stored in a database or retrieval system, without the prior written permission of the author and/or publisher. Printed in the United States.

Scriptures marked MSG are taken from the THE MESSAGE: THE BIBLE IN CONTEMPORARY ENGLISH (TM): Scripture taken from THE MESSAGE: THE BIBLE IN CONTEMPORARY ENGLISH, copyright©1993, 1994, 1995, 1996, 2000, 2001, 2002. Used by permission of NavPress Publishing Group

Scriptures marked NAS are taken from the NEW AMERICAN STANDARD (NASB/NAS): Scripture taken from the NEW AMERICAN STANDARD BIBLE®, copyright© 1960, 1962, 1963, 1968, 1971, 1972, 1973, 1975, 1977, 1995 by The Lockman Foundation. Used by permission.

Scriptures marked GNB are taken from the GOOD NEWS BIBLE (GNB/GNT): Scriptures taken from the Good News Bible ©1994 published by the Bible Societies/HarperCollins Publishers Ltd UK, Good News Bible© American Bible Society 1966, 1971, 1976, 1992. Used with permission.

Scriptures marked TLB are taken from the THE LIVING BIBLE (TLB): Scripture taken from THE LIVING BIBLE copyright© 1971. Used by permission of Tyndale House Publishers, Inc., Carol Stream, Illinois 60188. All rights reserved.

Scriptures marked ESV are taken from the THE HOLY BIBLE, ENGLISH STANDARD VERSION (ESV): Scriptures taken from THE HOLY BIBLE, ENGLISH STANDARD VERSION ® Copyright© 2001 by Crossway, a publishing ministry of Good News Publishers. Used by permission.

Scripture quotations marked NLV / NLT are taken from the Holy Bible, New Living Translation, copyright ©1996, 2004, 2015 by Tyndale House Foundation. Used by permission of Tyndale House Publishers, Carol Stream, Illinois 60188. All rights reserved.

Scriptures marked AMP are taken from the AMPLIFIED BIBLE (AMP): Scripture taken from the AMPLIFIED® BIBLE, Copyright © 1954, 1958, 1962, 1964, 1965, 1987 by the Lockman Foundation Used by Permission. (www.Lockman.org)

Scriptures marked KJV are taken from the KING JAMES VERSION (KJV): KING JAMES VERSION, public domain.

Scriptures marked NIV or NIRV are taken from the NEW INTERNATIONAL VERSION (NIV/NIRV): Scripture taken from THE HOLY BIBLE, NEW INTERNATIONAL VERSION ®. Copyright© 1973, 1978, 1984, 2011 by Biblica, Inc.™. Used by permission of Zondervan

Scriptures marked NKJV are taken from the NEW KING JAMES VERSION (NKJV): Scripture taken from the NEW KING JAMES VERSION®. Copyright© 1982 by Thomas Nelson, Inc. Used by permission. All rights reserved.

Scriptures marked ISV are taken from The Holy Bible: International Standard Version. Release 2.0, Build 2015.02.09. Copyright © 1995-2014 by ISV Foundation. ALL RIGHTS RESERVED INTERNATIONALLY. Used by permission of Davidson Press, LLC. Scripture quotations marked TPT are from The Passion Translation®. Copyright © 2017, 2018, 2020 by Passion & Fire Ministries, Inc. Used by permission. All rights reserved. ThePassionTranslation.com.

Published by:
Emerge Publishing, LLC
9521 Riverside Parkway, Suite 243 Tulsa, OK 74137 www.Emerge.pub
Library of Congress Cataloging-in-Publication Data:

ISBN: 978-1-954-966-25-3

Printed in the United States

Contents

Foreword By Tim Storey

In 2007, I received a call from a lady named Charese D. Sailor, who has since become like family to me. Her father, famous Detroit Lions Tight End Charlie Sanders, was going to be inducted into the Pro Football Hall Of Fame. Even though we had never met, his life got so touched by one of my books that she wanted to know if I would be willing to give a speech and surprise him on the day of his induction. I agreed happily. Little did I know that deciding to speak that day would lead to a lifelong relationship with such an amazing family.

After Charlie's induction, he told me how his daughter Charese had given him my book *Comeback and Beyond*. Its message had touched his life. Despite all his professional success, he also needed to make a comeback in other areas of his life.

As a best-selling author, I sincerely appreciate the power of messages to help and restore. When Charese told me about her book, I had to be a part of it. Why? Because her message can bring healing to your body, mind, and family. It can break your life's addiction, sadness, and shame. Finally, it can empower you to reset, restore, and reclaim your God-given purpose. It's finally time to go get your life. Let this message be a vehicle that will help get you there.

Introduction

I believe that each of us has earthly assignments given to us by our Heavenly Father. Maybe you are a woman who's also a mother, daughter, entrepreneur, leader, mentor, or pastor. Your divine assignment could be starting a church, raising a family, growing a business, or mentoring the next generation. Whatever God has called you to do—when you strive to accomplish His will for your life—He will position you to manifest the visions and dreams He's given you.

There's an old saying, "When you have an important mission, you can expect to encounter significant opposition." When we find ourselves stuck in a setback, we need assistance to get unstuck, stay on track, and keep our balance as we pursue our dreams and live out our purpose....on purpose. I wrote this book to do exactly that. This forty-day devotional journey is designed to help you restore, reset, and reclaim your God-given dreams.

Over the years, countless people have asked me how I was able to bounce back from the blindsides and plow through my setbacks. All who participate in the journey to reclaim, restore, and reset their dreams will do just that! This book is the sum total of my life lessons, broken down into compelling short stories and practical action steps designed to yield tangible daily results.

I hope that *Go Get Your Life!* will help you elevate and escalate your life in each of what I call the six "F's": Faith, Family, Finance, Fitness, Friends, and Fun.

Today is the day the rest of your life finally begins. The life you desire and deserve is within reach. It's time to Go Get Your Life!

MILE MARKERS

DAY ONE

*Friends, don't get me wrong: By no means do I count
myself an expert in all of this, but I've got my eye on the
goal, where God is beckoning us onward—to Jesus.
I'm off and running, and I'm not turning back.
So let's keep focused on that goal, those of us who want
everything God has for us. If any of you have something
else in mind, something less than total commitment, God
will clear your blurred vision - you'll see it yet!*
- Philippians 3:13-15 (MSG)

While life coaching some years ago, I encountered a client who had grown extremely frustrated with multiple failed attempts to lose weight. Despite her efforts, she remained on the diet roller coaster, fighting to exit the ride. Our conversation made it apparent that her true roadblock was not in finding an exit. It was a lack of *persistence* in the face of *resistance*. The only thing standing in her way was the challenge of staying consistent until her efforts produced change. She was the only one who had the power to fix it (2 Timothy 1:7)!

The more we uncovered, the more I realized she had a habit of starting and stopping short of her goals in many areas of her life. It was a pattern that developed from a personal fear of failure and disappointment. Even so, she still dared to try one more time.

During our first coaching session, she expressed that being fit for her upcoming birthday would be the perfect motivation she needed to stay the course this time. Curious, I asked when her birthday was, and she replied with a date five months away! A few weeks later, we formulated a realistic, sustainable plan. She became concerned that there wasn't enough time to reach her goals.

"That is more than enough time!" I told her encouragingly. "But you will have to stop looking so far down the road to a place you cannot yet see." "Instead," I explained, "Let's focus on the next ten days, then repeat until you arrive at your final destination"(Matthew 6:32).

As our sessions continued, I couldn't help but recognize the correlation between road trips and our journey during a physical, mental, or spiritual transformation. I have found that great travel companions are necessary on a long road trip. The conversations, sing-alongs, and games can help us move through the miles quickly as we pass each mile marker (Ecclesiastes 4:9).

Mile markers are small highway signs that show the number of miles you have traveled in a given direction. Mile markers have a way of easing weary travelers by keeping them mindful of their progress. Like road warriors on a long journey, we, too, should set our sights on mile markers along the pathway of life rather than becoming overwhelmed by long stretches. Instead of becoming discouraged during traffic or getting permanently stuck on a detour, pace yourself, lean in, and look up. You will soon recognize the meaningful progress you are making (Proverbs 4:25). If you can keep progressing, those small steps add up to a mile marker. Soon, the mile markers will complete the journey and remove the stress associated with *false failure*. The only way to fail is refusing to try, and when we are trying, that means we are actually doing. Take one day, one decision, and one step at a time. Even if the road may seem long, you are on it. Relax and keep moving in the right direction!

Definition Mile Marker/Milestone:

A series of numbered markers placed along a road or boundary at intervals of one mile or, occasionally, parts of a mile. They are typically located at the side of the road or in a median or central reservation. They are alternatively known as mile markers.

Prayer Before You Act:

Lord, I give my plans to you today, so you will establish them and reinforce my actions with discipline. I trust you will guide my course and order my steps as I accomplish the plans in my heart. Thank you in advance for removing mental roadblocks and physical distractions that would cause me to lose focus on my destination. Amen!

Action Step:

Today, set some mile markers for your life. Determine the direction you want to travel in and establish small goals you can accomplish every three to ten days. In your journal, mark the dates you intend to achieve these goals and set reminders on your phone. Check your progress when you hear the alerts. Every three-ten days, take a few minutes to review and give yourself credit for how far you've come.

MOVE ON

DAY TWO

Do not call to mind the former things or consider things of the past.
Behold, I am going to do something new, Now it will spring up;
Will you be aware of it? I will even make a roadway
in the wilderness, Rivers in the desert.
~ Isaiah 43:18-19 (NASB)

'Today is the day!' I exclaimed as I woke up for the last time in our cramped and somewhat dated home I shared with my husband and our three children. When we had enthusiastically purchased our first home, our kids were only seven, five, and four. At this point, they were all in high school. It was undoubtedly the time, if not overdue, to move into a bigger house!

That day we were about to begin a transformational move into a house worth four times our current home. As I packed, I realized that all five of us had shared one shower for the past eleven years. Files had overrun the basement and many other available areas. The living room had become my husband Marcus' office. The kitchen table doubled as an additional workspace space for my corner desk, which was also in the living room.

It was true. We had endured setbacks, poor choices, and business trials, which all led to moments of struggle and hardship. Yet, we never stopped believing we could improve our lives and create a legacy for our children and community (Proverbs 12:24).

Today was something to celebrate. We were about to begin a new season, empowered by many lessons learned along the way. No smell of smoke remained from those valuable, fiery trials (Daniel 3:27). Yet, we knew it was God's grace, not our hard work, that would launch us into a new season of abundance (2 Corinthians 12:9).

The more I thought about this new level of responsibility we were embarking on and all that had led to today, the more anxious and excited I became (Luke 12:48). Suddenly, I encountered an uneasy feeling, similar to car sickness, that overtook me.

The moving truck was outside, and all our boxes were packed! Everything was ready, so I wondered why I was feeling so hesitant.

I should have been elated! Our journey to find a new home had been nothing short of supernatural. After all, the house we were moving into had not even been for sale. The more I reflected, the more I realized my feelings of hesitation came from the fear of failing in this new season of our lives. It was a fear that, if left unchecked, had the potential to keep us cramped, both physically in this home and spiritually within our mindset (Isaiah 54:2).

Quickly, I acknowledged my fear and took inventory of the past failures that had spawned them. I also gave us credit for what we had achieved and how this move was evidence of that. Over the last ten years, we worked hard to break through old behavior patterns and set up new ways of moving forward. It was finally time to take the last step on this side of our breakthrough. That step could only be taken by realizing our new life was in this new home (Isaiah 43:19). I would have to trust that whatever challenges awaited us as a family in this new season, we would continue to grow and expand.

As I loaded the last few items into the truck, I could not believe everything we had accumulated over the years. Right until we taped the last box, these recurring questions rang in my ear: What do I take? What do I store? What can I use? What should I throw away?

We reviewed everything we owned in just a few weeks' time to decide what to keep or leave behind. Similarly, there were things we had carried in our hearts and minds for years that we also left behind because they had no place where we were going. We said goodbye to one season of our lives—which had seemed like a lifetime—and stepped into a new and better season. We were moving on. It was also when we exchanged our old mindset of scarcity for a Kingdom mindset of abundance (Ephesians 4:23). We were now ready to prosper where God was planting us.

Definition of Mindset:

An attitude, disposition, or mood, an intention or inclination

Prayer Before You Act:

Renew my heart and mind, Lord God, as I seek the release of old mindsets, people, and experiences that have held me captive. I thank you for the expansion necessary to accomplish every task, mission, and appointment you set for me at the foundation of the earth. In Jesus' name! Amen!

Action Step:

Today, clear out a drawer, closet, desk, or cabinet. Reflect on the things you need to leave behind and embrace the things you need with you as you move forward.

WHEN THE DUST CLEARS

DAY THREE

Has anyone by fussing before the mirror ever gotten taller by so much as an inch? If fussing can't even do that, why fuss at all? Walk into the fields and look at the wildflowers. They don't fuss with their appearance—but have you ever seen color and design quite like it? The ten best-dressed men and women in the country look shabby alongside them. If God gives such attention to the wildflowers, most of them never even seen, don't you think he'll attend to you, take pride in you, do his best for you?
~ Luke 12:27-28 MSG

One afternoon I was cleaning out a storage closet in my basement when I noticed several boxes stacked up in the far corner. I couldn't remember putting them there and hadn't seen them before. I abandoned the Christmas decorations I was sorting to take a closer look.

As I grabbed the first one, a thick layer of dusk swirled around me. This confirmed just how long the contents had been hidden in the corner waiting to be unpacked. At that point, I had no idea what was inside. The writing had faded on the outer labels, and the tape holding the box together had nearly disintegrated. As I pulled back the flaps to reach inside, I realized the box was full of memorabilia. Every dip my hand took made the box feel like a treasure chest. My heart dropped as I unwrapped trinkets connected to when my husband and I were just friends and transitioning into dating. I also discovered souvenirs from our honeymoon. Several items were cracked, broken, and weathered. The photos I saved had begun to curl around the edges. I also found our faded boarding passes and honeymoon suite key from the Bahamas. As I dug further, I found souvenirs in this box from adventure parks that the family and I had visited.

Finding these precious mementos brought back many memories of our family's humble and hopeful beginnings. They were like rare jewels that could never be recreated (Joel 2:25-26).

My husband and I began our journey as friends. Marcus and I became close when he generously helped my family and me through an unsteady time. When I started my business, Marcus was my rock and a source of constant support. In that season, it became clear that God had put us together for a reason. This box of keepsakes was evidence of all we had built, accomplished, and persevered through as a couple. It also made me realize how many goals and dreams surpassed our initial expectations.

"Wow!" I said as I opened a second box that kept awards my husband earned as a top producer in his early days of real estate. That season of abundance followed one of our most challenging seasons — closing our first salon in Lansing and having to move in with his parents. That was a tough time. However, it was a time that taught us lessons we needed in order to thrive in the future.

When you find yourself in the middle of a storm, it's easy to get caught up in the moment and lose a sense of perspective. As I reflected on our biggest losses and greatest wins, I wondered how many of our breakthroughs were overshadowed by my fits and fussing. Looking back, God had been faithful despite my shortcomings. He lavished me with grace and mercy every step of the way (Romans 11:29).

I learned much that day in the storage room; looking through different chapters of my life, I saw how faithful God truly is. It's incredible how nothing can stop God's plans for our lives. Despite our weaknesses and failures, he always comes through. I have learned that it's best to believe God's promises will happen and act as if it already has. Why? Because God is always faithful. Regardless of what you are going through, God is with you and watching over every promise He has given to you within His Word. (Jeremiah 1:12).

When we get impatient, we must remember that God's ways are not like ours. He won't lie to us like people sometimes do (Isaiah 55:8-9, Numbers 23:19). Scripture is very clear about what He intends to do for us. His will does not change (Hebrews 13:8). All we have to do is wipe off the dust to see the treasures of His faithful love beneath.

Definition of Faithfulness:

The fact or quality of being true to one's word or commitments as to what one has pledged to do and professes to believe.

Prayer Before You Act:

Dear Lord, just as easy as it is for me to dust off an old box to discover great treasures inside, help me shed beliefs and attitudes that hold me back. Empower me to uncover the treasures you have planted inside me. As I unpack dreams I have tucked away, please help me believe again. For you are faithful and will do what you said you would do. Help me not meddle with your perfect will. Help me let go of my frustrations and rest in your peace and love. Amen.

Action Step:

Pull out an old journal or vision board to see how far you have come. Applaud yourself for what you have done. Know that the best is yet to come. If our old dreams or visions have become dusty or dated, update them! With new fresh eyes, greater wisdom, and the breath of God, allow the manifestation of His promises to be furnished in your life today.

NO TRESPASSING ON THE PROCESS

DAY FOUR

A man's mind plans his way [as he journeys through life],
But the Lord directs his steps and establishes them.
- Proverbs 16:9 (AMP)

When I set out to pursue a career in broadcast journalism in 1989, I couldn't think of anything I wanted to do other than become an acclaimed news reporter and a voice for my community. For the most part, I enjoyed studying broadcast journalism and my college experience. I even made the dean's list a few times as an undergraduate. However, I eventually discovered that my true passion was entrepreneurship.

I was always a dreamer. After building a small business in college, I began believing I could create something big in the salon and spa industry. Immediately following graduation, I opened my first salon, My Sister's Shop. Established in 1996 near MSU's campus, the salon provided a professional space for other salon professionals to practice their craft and build their dreams.

When we opened My Sister's Shop, it instantly became popular on campus. We regularly shuttled students from the dorms to the salon and sold deli sandwiches as patrons waited. We helped several people become licensed practitioners through our apprenticeship program. I held nail art seminars and sold my instructional videos to customers all over the globe. My work was even featured in Nail Art Magazine and Airbrush Action. The salon became a huge success.

Even though I was only in my twenties, I remember many days when I felt impatient and frustrated. Yes, I was happy about my early success and the financial independence we created. However, serving clients, meeting the administrative demands of a small business, and managing employees proved incredibly challenging. As a young leader, I suffered through ridicule and betrayal that tested my faith, patience, and sanity. I began to wonder if I had made the right decision to open my own small business instead of getting a regular job. Unfortunately, the vacillation only opened the door to more doubt (Proverbs 28:26). I began thinking things like "I should be further along by now" and "Success can't be this hard." I even began to question God, saying "You told me to dream, so why does it feel like such a burden?"

Thankfully, my husband was a force for hope and optimism whenever I felt pressure. When I would get too low, he would pick me up and exchange my negative words for positive ones (Ephesians 4:3). Marcus fully supported me, even forfeiting law school to help me build my dream. When I began to share my self-doubt with him, he would say the words of a true Sailor, "Batten down the hatches!" That was his way of reminding me not to let fear into my spirit or waver in uncertainty (James 1:8).

Building a business from the ground up is hard work. Sometimes it's even downright frustrating. However, if you're not careful, you can let your frustration rob you of enjoying the process. As I matured, I eventually learned the power of trust. Whether you like it or not, the process is necessary before you can truly step into what God has for you. These steps are necessary and ordered by God (Psalm 37:23). This is why you must choose joy, especially when you want to complain (James 1:2-6).

Looking back, the biggest mistake I made was being impatient. Even though my salon was growing, I felt it wasn't growing fast enough. Instead of focusing on my core business, I began wasting my time on side projects. My first venture was a networking company. When that failed to gain traction, I joined another. Then another. After five different attempts, I did not find success. No matter how many other secondary businesses I launched, I always returned to my original idea. Eventually, it hit me. What if God had already put me on a path to my desired success? I had wasted years of time and money on projects that didn't pan out. In reality, the key to my professional success was in front of me the whole time. I had let distractions trespass on the land God had given me, and it was affecting my harvest.

My good friend Tim Storey says, "There is a difference between a good idea and a God idea." When good ideas come, it's easy to lose focus on our God idea. If you're not careful, good ideas can rob you of fully achieving the God idea for your life. When distractions trespass on your dreams, make the decision to say no. Be strong and trust in the Lord. Know that there is a process to what God wants to do in and through you. When you trust the process, you will reap the harvest God has prepared for you (Galatians 6:9).

Over the years, Marcus and I have owned and operated thirteen salons and salon suites. We now oversee five locations housing more than fifty suites. As the nationwide salon suite forerunners, we have strived to follow our salon's vision statement, "A Professional Establishment for the Established Professional." Despite the incredible competition of our salons located in the "Hair and Nail Capital of the World," we have always been at least 97% full from inception. I believe a large part of our success is attributed to our company culture of treating everyone in the way we want to be treated (Luke 6:31).

When I started my professional journey, I did not expect to end up in the salon industry. But with each breakthrough came confirmation that I was in the place God had prepared for me (Deuteronomy 11:9). In the same vein, the closed doors were indicators that I may be trespassing in areas that were not for me. Eventually, when I learned to remain in the land God had prepared, doors of opportunity and provision began to open. That is my story. First, it seemed adventurous and risky. By no means was it easy, but God knew what future Charese would need. Because I stayed the course, I'm now living what was once a dream in college. By following the path to the land that was made for me, I've been able to help others travel to their promised land as well.

In due time, He always elevates those who serve Him (1 Peter 5:6). It's amazing how God's plan and timing are always perfect! Let His process grow your faith, and His blessings reflect His glory in every part of your life (Psalm 31:15). As you wait on Him without trespassing, you will one day enter into the great things He has prepared for you.

Definition of Process:
Treat or prepare by some particular systematic series of actions to achieve a specific end.

Prayer Before You Act:
Dear God, thank you for lighting my path today and every day. Continue to reveal the road you have designed for me to walk on, so I will be blessed, prosperous, and healthy. I desire to reach the places You have prepared for me. Even if I don't always understand the process, I trust You will be with me and keep me on the path. Amen!

Action Step:
Reflect on the last opportunity you had. What was the opportunity? If the opportunity turned out well, what signs or open doors confirmed you were on the right path? If the opportunity turned out poorly, what were the closed doors that confirmed your steps were trespassing on the land God did not have for you?

SEASONS CHANGE

DAY FIVE

*But now the Lord who created you, O Israel, says: Don't be
afraid, for I have ransomed you; I have called you by name; you
are mine. When you go through deep waters and great trouble,
I will be with you. When you go through rivers of difficulty, you
will not drown! When you walk through the fire of oppression,
you will not be burned up-the flames will not consume you.*
~ Isaiah 43:1-2 (TLB)

Having lived in Michigan my whole life, I don't think wearing a jacket
in June or shorts in November is unusual. Though the seasons may
change, the weather can have its own agenda, especially in the mitten-
shaped state. After the leaves have fallen to the ground, everyone knows
it's time for winter. Though we prepare every year by changing our tires
and wardrobes, the brutal Michigan winters always catch us off guard.

Sometimes life brings surprise storms: a bad report from the doctor, a
breakup, or an unexpected bill. I've learned that God uses these storms
to launch us into our divine destiny. When we are tempted to give up,
hold onto God's Word. It will sustain you through difficult seasons.

During my first year of college, I was blindsided by an unexpected tuition bill that, if not paid, would force me to drop out of MSU. I was determined to find the money. Every day I diligently looked for work but never received a callback. With the future of my college enrollment uncertain, I did everything I could to find a way to stay in school. I negotiated with financial aid, reached out to my guidance counselor, and sent emails to the administration. After exhausting my available options, I still could not find a way forward.

One day I had a novel idea while spending a quiet moment alone. I thought about how, since arriving on campus, people frequently stopped to compliment me on my signature nail art. They told me they would love to have nails like mine but could not afford it on a student's budget. The next day I hung a sign on my dorm room letting others know I was open for business as a nail artist. I promoted my new services by offering special discounts to students who lived on campus using my tagline "Nail Art Bringing the Motor City to Your Town."

My fellow college students loved it! Soon my small business ignited an inner passion for entrepreneurship that still burns within me today. It didn't take long until I entered a cosmetology apprenticeship program to increase my business income. As I gained experience as a manicurist, I became a better nail artist and increased my clientele. There were days when I worked six-eight hours between classes. I was determined to finish my degree and not lose sight of realizing my goals and dreams.

It's incredible that a financial storm I never saw coming led me to find my passion as a businesswoman. It taught me how to make it through times of scarcity and steward times of abundance. Over time the lessons I learned empowered me to open my own beauty salons and become the forerunner of the salon suite model. It also instilled an inner confidence that would help me navigate rough seasons throughout my life (2 Corinthians 4:17-18).

When we're headed into a storm, it's easy to feel insecure, uneasy, and unsteady. However, even in hurricane weather, God's Word can be our place of peace. His promises always remain even when the future looks uncertain (Matthew 24:35). His grace takes our mess and turns it into a message.

Storms uncover or blow away dead things in our lives. Every cloud has a silver lining, but we often won't see it until it passes. Mine was the desire to stay in school that turned into financial freedom.

After experiencing 30 years of weathering storms, I can promise there is a blessing in your current storm. In fact, the wind might take you to places and spaces you never thought possible (Ephesians 3:20). Do not fret when a new storm blows into your life.

Take shelter, take heart, listen closely, and remember "This too shall pass." Storms always do. In the end it might even leave a rainbow.

Definition of Storm:

A violent atmospheric disturbance with strong winds, usually rain, thunder, lightning, or snow. An explosive reaction, an uproar, or controversy.

Prayer Before You Act:

Dear God, I know you have been with me through every storm I have ever weathered. As I continue to make plans for my future, I trust that any change you allow to happen will work in my favor because I love you. Give me continual peace in the eye of the storm, so that I can rise above the turbulence.

Action Step:

Has a recent, unexpected storm shown up in your life, causing you to abruptly change directions from where you were headed? What was the silver lining in it or the rainbow that showed up afterward? Did it cause you to use a dormant skill or discover one you didn't know you had? How could your experience manifest into a business, book, manual, hobby, or support group? How can you take your experience and use your test to be a testimony to others? Take five to ten minutes and answer these questions in a journal today.

ALREADY THERE

DAY SIX

"But you must be strong and not be discouraged.
The work that you do will be rewarded."
~ 2 Chronicles 15:7 (GNT)

As I watched my reflection in the gym wall mirror during my elliptical workout, I noticed I had gained a few pounds since my last visit. Rolls were forming on my sides, and my thighs had begun to touch again. As someone who has struggled with weight for years, I immediately regretted my recent food choices. I began to beat myself up, thinking about how long it would take to fix this. Then, I heard a voice in my head say, "You are already there!"

I quietly said to myself, "Yes, Charese, you *are* already there!" Again and again, I said this to myself as I continued to work out. Those declarations became a mantra reminding me how much I had accomplished. I knew the Covid weight gain did not only affect me. 40% of Americans had gained twelve to twenty-eight pounds as well. I also knew that if I put in the work and focused on performing the proper daily habits, I could shed the weight as fast as I had put it on.

Over the last few decades, I have transformed my body, lost 156 pounds, and coached hundreds to do the same. I knew how to break the cycle of stress eating. It was going to take the right mindset to get back on track, break my new negative feedback loops, and go get the life I wanted again.

Sometimes when we experience a setback, we break free by visualizing our comeback before it happens. Colossians 3:2 tells us to "Set our minds on things above, not on things that are on Earth." Yes, it was true I had gained a considerable amount of weight. However, I had to focus my mind and energy on where I wanted to be. I had to believe I was "already there." All that was left was for me to realize it through action.

God gave us the ability to dream. Dreaming is the ability to visualize our ideal future for ourselves and those we love. Whenever I begin coaching new clients, the first task I give them is writing out a vision for their lives. Why? The written vision holds them accountable for what they plan to accomplish (Habakkuk 2:2-3).

Yes, you might not have reached your goals yet, but if you begin to operate as though you already have, you will arrive sooner and enjoy yourself along the way. If you are going to seize it, you have to first see it. Even if it hasn't materialized, hold onto the hope that the vision will suddenly become your reality (Hebrews 11:1).

To properly focus your vision, you have to give up the practice of second-guessing yourself. Secondly, you have to be willing to push back against the inner thoughts that beat you up. Finally, you must be ready to love yourself unconditionally and believe you are worth fighting for.

All too often, we become overwhelmed by the long journey in front of us. The finish line can seem so far away that we grow weary before we begin. However, if you believe you are worth it, you can push through negative thoughts that can lead to setbacks and self-sabotage. The more you believe in yourself, the easier it will be to evaluate your inner dialogue.

That means rejecting negative thoughts that hurt you and accepting positive thoughts that encourage you.

That's what it means to believe you are "already there." You are already the person that can achieve your dreams. You are already worthy enough to receive love, praise, and support. You are already blessed and a blessing to others. You are already powerful and capable. You already have everything you need to become the real you. Now, all that's left is to go get your life.

Definition of There:

In, at, or to that place or position. Used in attracting someone's attention or calling attention to someone or something.

Prayer Before You Act:

Dear Heavenly Father, help me achieve the things I set out to do even when I fall short while getting there. Enable me to quench self-doubt and reject every lie that delays my arrival. Let my mind be renewed as I focus on Your goodness. Let Your Word empower me, for I am more than a conqueror in You. With your help, I will realize the dreams you have given me. Amen!

Action Step:

Take a few minutes to identify one of your personal or professional goals. Maybe you want to lose weight, start a new business, or learn a new language. Once you do, write down one simple step you can take daily that will empower you to achieve it. Write down your step on a post-it note and place it somewhere you will see daily to remind you to go get your life.

LAY OUT

DAY SEVEN

"Enlarge the place of your tent, and let the curtains of your habitations be stretched out; do not hold back; lengthen your cords and strengthen your stakes."
~ Isaiah 54:2 (ESV)

My father, Charlie Sanders, was known in the NFL for his willingness to sacrifice his body and make acrobatic catches during critical plays. His rare ability to block, tackle, and catch along with his unmatched work ethic granted him notoriety. In 2007, he was inducted into the NFL Hall of Fame as one of six tight ends to ever be elected. This career-defining honor came after years of dedication, preparation, and motivation despite many obstacles, barriers, and setbacks (Romans 8:37).

As a child, my father experienced some challenges that deeply wounded him. When he was just two years old, his mother died while giving birth to his youngest brother. He was raised by his stepmother, whom he honored, but she often had a sharp tone and a cold demeanor (Exodus 20:12). There were other hardships that touched his life, but the very things that caused him to be stretched mentally, emotionally, and spiritually made him stronger (1 Peter 5:10). They strengthened his faith in God and taught him how to lean on the Lord in every season.

My dad also had great role models. His father was an accomplished professor who taught him the value of hard work, intelligence, and dedication. His grandfather was a reverend and showed him the importance of living with faith. He also instilled in my father the importance of higher education and gave him opportunities to work on the family farm. These early experiences inspired my father to make hard work his lifelong friend and to remain humble despite success. In every situation, he would always do things with excellence, knowing God had graced him with his abilities (Psalm 128:2).

The mental fortitude he developed early on prepared him for greatness and to become one of the best tight ends in football history. At the height of his career, he was able to say those two famous words athletes dream of saying," Hi, Mom!" He could never actually stare into the camera from a stadium and give his mom honor during his career due to her passing. He did, however, address his mom in heaven in a touching moment during his induction ceremony. That day he delivered a speech that has become one of the most-watched NFL Hall of Fame speeches of all time. There was not a dry eye in the audience as the commentator sniffled and transitioned into a commercial break.

Despite it all, he had turned his childhood dreams into reality. He experienced it during the biggest stage of his career as he was dawned with the yellow jacket worn by the few who made it into the NFL Hall of Fame. I'd like to think he received beauty for ashes (Isaiah 61:3).

Life is full of surprises that require us to adjust constantly. It makes it feel like we are rerouting plans most days. Other times our plans can appear to work perfectly. Refuse to throw in the towel when things don't go as planned.

Like a football team huddling after a play and calling an audible, learn to huddle with the Holy Spirit (John 14:26). In every situation, go to God. Ask for his counsel and wisdom to make adjustments and redirect your focus.

In life, you will have to lay out, stretch, speed up, and even slow down to reach your dreams. Sometimes you have to create a new path forward. Even while he was in motion and the enemy team was trying to tackle him, my dad had to trust the quarterback to throw the ball at the right time. We also must trust God, who is quarterbacking our lives with timing and precision.

In my father's last interview, just days before he passed away, he told the news, "I'm going to kick cancer's butt!" Why? Because he believed to the end, he could overcome whatever stood in his way. That was how he played the game of football and lived his life. We may not make it to the Pro Football Hall of Fame like my father, The Great 88, but we each have a level of greatness we were born to achieve (Philippians 3:14).

Be inspired to stretch, adjust, reroute, grow, and repeat until the play is complete. Just keep running your route no matter how many times you are tackled by the difficulties of life.

Definition of Lay Out:
Spread something out to its full extent, especially to be seen. Construct or arrange (buildings or gardens) according to a plan.

Prayer Before You Act:
Dear God, Thank you for making me victorious and creating me to win in every area of my life. Thank you for giving me the patience I need to complete the play. Thank you for always giving me chances to try again. Empower me to reclaim, reset, and restore the dreams you've given me. Amen.

Action Step:
Think of one or two desires you have tried to complete but are being constantly rerouted. Identify obstacles that are hindering you from moving forward. It can be as simple as cleaning out your refrigerator or as large as buying a new home. Ask yourself, "Is there a new play you can run to avoid or eliminate the opposition?" Huddle with the Holy Spirit and ask Him to give you wisdom and counsel this season.

ARE YOU OK?

DAY EIGHT

"The Lord is gracious and righteous; our God is full of compassion.
The Lord protects the unwary; when I was brought low, he saved me."
~ Psalm 116:5-6

OK can be used to express many things. It's an answer to a question, and sometimes is the question itself. In other instances, OK can both pacify or exaggerate something. This common phrase is also offered to encourage someone. Still, it can be used as a nonchalant expression of discouragement in moments when we are not OK.

OK is also too commonly used as a mask for the true answer to "How are you doing?" It can be a word that prevents intimacy and vulnerability.

When dating my husband, I remember him never accepting OK as a response from me. He would often say, "OK, never means OK." When he would challenge me to elaborate, I initially felt scrutinized. However, over time I realized it was his attempt to listen and understand what I was truly saying and what I needed. His questions also made me mindful of my personal defense mechanisms. Why would I say I was OK when I really wasn't? What was I avoiding, and what parts of me needed healing?

Looking back, it's clear God used my husband to help me heal from years of emotional terrorism, the result of the hard times I faced growing up that led to self-sabotage later in life. That same pain drove me to binge eat my way to 320 pounds in my early 20s. I thank God Marcus was patient enough to love me through it all.

It's easy to use the word OK to mask the pain we feel in life. Maybe you've been hurt in a relationship, and you're in desperate need of healing. Maybe you're overworked and undervalued, and you desire restoration. Whatever the case may be, it's time to step out of the land of your OK and into the future God wants to take you.

That's the beauty of God. He will never leave you in your OK. Instead, He wants you to be OK in Him. He wants you to live fully unstuck from your past and redeemed in Him. He wants you to live in a position of power, safety, and security. Despite the chaos of life, you can still be unshakable. You can have peace because God is walking with you and carrying your burdens (1 Peter 5:7). When things are genuinely dark, He promises to be your light along the road to restoration, repair, and rehabilitation (Psalm 119:10).

Definition of Balance:

An even weight distribution enabling someone or something to remain upright and steady. A condition in which different elements are equal or in the correct proportions.

Prayer Before You Act:

God, I thank you for your guidance every day. You have promised to never leave nor forsake me. You lead me through tough times when I don't know the way. Thank you for healing my heart from the past and surrounding me with those who seek to help me. Give me the ears to hear You clearly and the obedience to follow You swiftly. Amen

Action Step:

View yourself OK in an area of your life in which you may have been unsteady or insecure recently. Release any fear, anxiety, or uncertainty. God is in control. He is with you in the high or low places. He has the solutions to bring balance and make everything that concerns us OK. Take a moment to listen for His voice inside of you and write out the answers. I believe He will speak to your spirit as a result of today's prayer and meditation.

BLOW YOUR HOUSE DOWN

DAY NINE

*These words I speak to you are not incidental additions
to your life, homeowner improvements to your standard
of living. They are foundational words, words to build a
life on. If you work these words into your life, you are like
a smart carpenter who built his house on solid rock.
Rain poured down, the river flooded, a tornado hit - but
nothing moved that house. It was fixed to the rock.
~ Matthew 7: 24-25 (MSG)*

"The Three Little Pigs" is a fable written in 1890 about three pigs who build three houses out of different materials. The Big Bad Wolf blows down the first two homes made of straw and sticks but cannot destroy the third pig's house built out of bricks.

It's amazing how a strong structure built from the right materials can weather even the greatest storms. In the case of the third pig, the story is clear. His use of bricks to construct his house meant he could protect himself from the Big Bad Wolf. What the story doesn't say is that if it had not been for the mortar, the bricks would have never stayed together.

Mortar is a mixture of lime, cement, sand, and water. It is used in the bonding of bricks. It is an essential ingredient to building a strong, sturdy structure.

In life, there are things that huff and puff at us and threaten to blow our lives down. Like the third little pig, we, too can construct our lives to weather any storm. Where others learn through trial and error, we can stand on God's Word no matter what threats come against us. His promises can feed our faith and starve our doubts.

God has given us not only the proper raw materials in the form of biblical wisdom and promises but also the glue to hold it together—the Holy Spirit. Just like the mortar, the Holy Spirit holds everything in place. His voice guides us as things come to huff and puff and blow our lives down (John 16:13). The Holy Spirit is the Wonderful Counselor. He will teach you all you need to know. Just the mortar that held the third house together, the Holy Spirit will help you keep it together when life becomes difficult.

That's the power of living aligned with the Holy Spirit. When we choose to live with His wisdom, and by His power, we build a strong foundation for our own lives and become a refuge for others. In other words, God's refuge becomes our refuge. When we find strength in Him in times of trouble, we become a wellspring to those whose houses were blown down (Psalm 46:1-3).

Constructing your life on a firm foundation is a partnership between the Holy Spirit and you. In times of trial, He is your helper and comforter. In times of chaos, He will fill you with peace and give you wisdom. Like mortar, He fills your voids even when unaware of what needs to be held together. In the space where you lack patience, He is patient for you. When you find yourself confused or suffering from self-doubt, He fills your insecurities with knowledge and insight. He will always give you the right words when you don't know how or what to pray for. Why? The Holy Spirit is gracious. He will gradually fill every empty space in your life and hold you together. He is the glue that makes everything whole again and fixes what is broken (Psalm 116: 5-6).

Definition of Bond:

Join or be joined securely to something else, especially by means of an adhesive substance, heat, or pressure.

Prayer Before You Act:

God, thank you for holding everything together in my life even when the winds blow. When the enemy threatens my life, status, loved ones, or dreams, you are my protection. You keep it all safe and always restore me as I abide in you. Let the storm in my life strengthen me and my bond with you. Tell me what I need to know by your Spirit so I can continue to build my life for your glory. Amen.

Action Step:

There are fifty-eight bible verses in scripture about wind. Sometimes the wind is sent from God; other times, the wind comes from storms. When the wind blows, are you building your house without mortar, or are you building your life on God's Word? Here are five simple questions you can use to help you apply biblical wisdom to your life:

1. What winds have erupted over the past twelve months? (Name 1-3)

2. Was the wind something that changed your direction, or did it stop you in your tracks?

3. Do you feel God allowed the wind? If so, Why?

4. Is there anything you could have had in place to brace yourself for the wind?

5. Did you utilize the Holy Spirit through exercising any Fruits of the Spirit?

6. Did you use a strategy brought to you by the Holy Spirit of God to stay glued and grounded during these winds?

JUST DO IT!

DAY TEN

"For the vision is yet for the appointed [future] time
It hurries toward the goal [of fulfillment]; it will not fail.
Even though it delays, wait [patiently] for it,
because it will certainly come; it will not delay.
~ Habakkuk 2:3 (AMP)

One evening I sneaked up to my room with the intention of working on one of my books. I had been writing this particular manuscript for much longer than I anticipated, and deadlines were looming. It had become difficult to find pockets of time to write with three active children and a growing business.

Depending on the unforeseen needs of my family and the pop-up urgencies of a business, I knew my timeline might need to be adjusted. I was determined to isolate myself for a few hours each day and finish the book. As I opened my bedroom door, I was greeted with a mound of laundry blocking my writing area. Immediately, my optimism faded. I quickly began sorting, folding, and hanging. I burned up almost all the time I had set aside to write.

I was becoming increasingly irritated with every article of clothing I touched because my time—once again—was being compromised. All of a sudden, the million-dollar phrase coined by Nike rang in my head," JUST DO IT!"

Abruptly, I shoved the remaining clothes onto the floor. "These clothes are going to get dirty, washed, rinsed, and dirtied again," I thought to myself. "But I will never recover this particular time and space."

At that moment, the burden of responsibility as a homemaker needed to be released (Psalm 55:22). While keeping a tidy home was necessary, I could not sacrifice the future for the present. As I picked up a pen to write, I was reminded that certain assignments require more urgency than others. It also was true that the most urgent assignments always seemed to be the most distracting. Behind every great reward is great resistance.

Similar to how companies provide bonuses for performance, we also reap the rewards upon completing goals. Procrastination, even when masked by productivity, robs us of the time meant for completing goals and the accompanying rewards. This does not mean the assignment can't be completed after the time frame passes, but at some point, a window may close and change the intended outcome (John 9:4).

If you can discipline yourself to just do it, your assignments won't be found lying around like loads of laundry. That's the downside of overthinking. When you wait too long to act, your thoughts can distract you. If you're not careful, they can cause you to get stuck and miss the breakthrough God has already prepared for you.

God is calling you to finish what you have started. He desires to give you more on top of what you have already built. However, he can only bless you according to what you are willing to receive. When you take care of what you've been given and complete the tasks you've been assigned, you make room for more.

Whatever your specific assignment or dream you have, just do it! Even if you're insecure, unsure, or doubt yourself, just do it! If you are tired and weary, just do it! You are stronger than you think you are. His power has now become your strength (Ephesians 6:10). Keep going, keep pushing, and keep moving forward. In every step you take, God is with you (Joshua 1:9).

Definition of Time-frame:

A period of time, especially a specified period in which something occurs or is planned to occur.

Prayer Before You Act:

Dear God, thank you for helping me to understand time-frames and seasons. Thank you for the wisdom and resources to complete the assignments you have ordained over my life so that I can be all you have called me to be. Help me be ready to receive every reward you predestined for me. Amen.

Action Step:

Is there something you have been meaning to do for a while but have been putting off? Maybe you need to clear out a chest of drawers, hang some pictures, or read a helpful book like *Go Get Your Life!*? Maybe you need to write your own book and change lives with your story? JUST DO IT! Journal your progress at fourteen, twenty-eight, and forty days. If distractions have caused any delay, notate them and resist them when they show up again.

"Somebody is waiting on the other side of your obedience"- Tim Storey.

AGONY OF DEFEAT

DAY ELEVEN

We are often troubled, but not crushed; sometimes in doubt, but never in despair; there are many enemies, but we are never without a friend; and though badly hurt at times, we are not destroyed.
~ 2 Corinthians 4:8-9 (GNT)

After a gut-wrenching loss to my son's rivals in the game's final seconds, we exited the fieldhouse, sauntering behind the football team. That evening was a defining game that attracted several college scouts. It also was supposed to be the start of another championship season. The game's match-up would have earned a student-athlete a college scholarship with the proper performance. Several players began to walk in a different direction instead of taking the traditional march into the locker room. They eventually huddled outside the football field's fence in the parking lot. All the players were visibly upset. The pain of losing a game they had worked so hard to win was too fresh for them to have a post-game analysis.

As I walked closer, I noticed one young man was experiencing the "agony of defeat" more intensely than the rest. It was Richie, the new team member who transferred last year. Due to eligibility rules, he had to anxiously wait on the sidelines the previous season before playing in that evening's game. Despite touching the ball while attempting to make an interception, he'd missed the game-winning pick on the final play! He had thwarted the team's last chance to win.

As I got closer to the huddle, the entire parking lot turned toward me as I yelled, "Hey! Is that my favorite player, Richie!?" playfully. He walked toward me with tears flowing and sobbed into my shoulder. Gently, I lifted his head, looked him square in the eyes, and told him, "This is the agony of defeat. Though it's piercing, it is also the price when we go all out for a win and still somehow lose. So keep your head up and prepare to win again" (Proverbs 4:25-27).

"Thank You, Mrs. Sailor!" he exclaimed. "You are right. This is just the first game, and I need to focus on next week's opponent." At that moment, he saw the bigger picture (Isaiah 46:10-11). Life is not a sprint; it's a marathon. One loss could not define his efforts over an entire season. However, if he could stay patient and keep improving, he would be ready for victory during the playoffs. (Proverbs 14:29).

When disappointments appear in our lives, we must be careful to reject discouragement. It causes us to lose sight of the bigger purpose attached to the smaller plans (James 1:2).

Even if it looks like something was lost—when we come through and dry our eyes—those experiences produce wisdom and knowledge. Only through failure can we learn to rise again, press on, and take another shot at hitting the mark (Philippians 3:14). Put another way, overcoming adversity fosters mental toughness.

Mental toughness is a term my father coined and applied during his decade playing for the Detroit Lions. He was known for playing through pain and sacrificing his body for the win with very little concern about the hits he took. He remained mentally tough because he understood the assignment and didn't allow anything to interfere. Like my father, we, too, have to work through the pain while taking the hits as we are striving to win at life.

When we turn our messes into messages, and our tests into testimonies, we increase our mental toughness. When you gain understanding like Richie did and focus on winning the long game, you put yourself in the best position to always come out ahead (Proverbs 4:7)!

Despite what trials you might go through, you must remember that you are more than a conqueror through Christ who loves you unconditionally. Thanks be to God that you are triumphant and have already been given the victory in Him (Romans 8:37, 2 Corinthians 2:14, 1 Corinthians 15:57).

Know that there is a master plan at work that you cannot always see with your natural eyes. We often fail to consider that there will be unexpected twists and turns between the starting and finish lines of the races we run. There is also nothing that can stop those plans that have been ordered by God or separate us from His love (Psalm 33:11, Romans 8:38-39). Just like Richie and his teammates discovered, defeat may feel final at the moment. However, the sting of loss will pass away. What will be left will be a more resilient, knowledgeable, and capable version of yourself that God is preparing to do great things in and through.

Definition of Mental Toughness:
A measure of individual resilience and confidence that may predict success in sports, education, and the workplace. As a broad concept, mental toughness initially emerged in the context of sports training. It's a set of attributes that allows a person to become a better athlete through coping with difficult training and competitive situations.

Prayer Before You Act:
I can do all things through You who strengthens me. When I feel defeated or

hurt, help me to remember that I am being made stronger through it. Every trial I face is an opportunity to become better, not bitter. Empower me to be mentally tough and resilient in every season. Reveal to me the path You have already prepared for me so that I might always be victorious. Amen.

Action Step:

First, take five to ten minutes and write down the last time you struggled with mental toughness. Take note of how you felt when you couldn't handle the pressure. What was your response or reaction? Did you stress eat, impulsively shop, or lose your temper? Was there something going on in your life at that time that had you stressed? Were you lacking sleep or overworked that day? All of these circumstances compromise our mental toughness. Secondly, write down the last time you were mentally tough in the face of adversity! Let your wins serve as a reminder of how capable you really are. Regardless of the battle, you can deal with difficult situations, keep the peace and emerge confidently.

UNLOAD

DAY TWELVE

Pile your troubles on God's shoulders—he'll carry your load,
he'll help you out. He'll never let good people topple into ruin.
~ Psalm 55:22-23 (MSG)

On the same Sunday every year, my family and I leave church early and quickly rush home. Over a span of a few hours, over 400 guests will attend the annual Legacy Tea hosted by my friend Lynn Johnson and her organization, Gathering Friends for TLC, to honor and support women. It's an event I look forward to every year. In the last ten years, I've only missed it once.

On this particular Sunday, I cooked dinner early and prepared everything so my family could attend the event. This included laying out my children's pajamas, correcting their homework, completing their backpack checks, and shampooing our daughter's hair the night before.

I was very excited to gather with other women in our tea-time attire and celebrate. Hundreds of beautiful vintage tea cups adorned the linen-covered tables. As I got dressed, I realized I had forgotten to pick up the hat I was planning to wear. This particular hat was very important to me. It was a gift from my late mother-in-law and was being restored so I could wear it in her honor.

"How could I have forgotten to do the most important task on my to-do list?" I wondered aloud. As I pondered whether or not to pick up my hat on the way to the tea, sticky notes posted to my vanity caught my attention. My husband playfully calls this the "Sticky Note Garden" because the amount of Post-It notes always seems to grow. One note, in particular, caught my eye. It read, "Science project supplies due on Monday." Unfortunately, I couldn't remember which Monday.

My plan to take care of my family before leaving for the tea was quickly falling apart. After confirming the children's supplies were indeed needed in the morning, a wave of disappointment rushed over me.

 I concluded that I needed to cancel my plans before suddenly hearing one simple word echo in the distance of my mind. Unload.

I heard it so clearly that I first wondered if my Alexa device was reminding me to unload the dishes. It was actually my inner voice reminding me that I had taken too much on.

Instead of canceling my plans, I needed to take a moment and actively articulate what was causing me to feel anxious (Philippians 4:6-7). I had to slow down and remind myself that I had total control over the situation. No one was forcing me to do everything on my to-do list. Responsibilities could be adjusted. Dinner could have been ordered in, and I didn't have to wear my special hat this year. As for the science project supplies, only the materials were due, not the finished project. I could ask my husband Marcus to take on that burden or tell the teacher it would be late.

When you feel anxious or overwhelmed, the simple process of pausing, reflecting, and re-prioritizing is a powerful three-step exercise that will lighten your load (Isaiah 52:12). This is especially true when we prioritize our to-do list to line up with our life's purpose.

Go-getters, who are givers of their time, talent, and treasure, are really go-givers. Why? It's easy to take on so much in the pursuit of giving that we can be left feeling lopsided.

When we find ourselves overwhelmed, we can choose to release our burdens to God and ask for help from others. God cares about us and wants us to give our worries to Him (1 Peter 5:7). When the load you are carrying feels the heaviest; I guarantee your relief is near. Miraculous help will show up to rescue you in the nick of time (2 Corinthians 6:2).

When our burden is heavy, it's also time to take inventory of what we carry. We should analyze what responsibilities should remain and which ones can be eliminated. When we lighten our load, we create space for thoughtful execution and meaningful follow-through of what we are called to carry and complete.

That Sunday afternoon, I was reminded that God never gives us more than we can bear. He knows what we can handle and wants us to enjoy our lives. For me, enjoyment meant attending a gathering full of women who were encouragers to one another (1 Thessalonians 5:11).

As a person who is responsible for much, it's important to remember your load limits. You must learn your load limit and practice giving God what you can't carry. Like a truck that stops at checkpoints to weigh in and ensure its load is under the weight limit, you must regularly check in with God to be sure you don't topple over (Isaiah 46:4, Matthew 11:28-30).

Definition of Load:

Noun: A heavy or bulky thing that is carried or about to be carried. A weight or source of pressure borne by someone or something.

Verb: Make (someone or something) carry or hold a large or excessive amount of heavy things.

Prayer Before You Act:

Father, thank you for the capacity to do great and mighty things by your grace! Open my eyes and sharpen my discernment as I sort through and discard any unnecessary load. I desire to be effective for myself and those I love. Amen.

Action Step:

Think about what is weighing you down and needs to be unloaded. Could it be a relationship, a bill, or an unfulfilled promise you made to yourself? Once you've identified it, write down how it makes you feel and place a bookmark in your journal so you can refer back over the coming week. For the next 7 days, commit to setting aside what burdens you and ask for help.

KEEP YOUR EYES ON THE HORIZON

DAY THIRTEEN

Instead of shame and dishonor, you will enjoy a double share of honor.
You will possess a double portion of prosperity in your land,
and everlasting joy will be yours.
~ Isaiah 61:7 (NLV)

Still adjusting to jet lag while visiting my niece in California, I was awoken by the sun peeking through the blinds. I decided to step outside on the apartment balcony for a closer look at Westwood Village. Memories of my past flashed before my eyes. I began reflecting deeply on a not-so-pleasant time in my life when I was in this area years before. Between my sophomore and junior years of high school, my mother entered my younger siblings into a track and field program at UCLA. I was too old to participate, so I had to relocate with the rest of the family to support them that summer.

While living there, I took a job working at Sizzler. The commute by public transportation was at least an hour each way. I often found myself alone, in the dark, and sometimes traveling through areas of Los Angeles I should not have been in.

As I reminisced, I noticed a familiar movie theater in the distance on the horizon. I realized it was the same movie theater where my mother took us to see the premier of *La Bamba*. It was a movie that gave me courage and inspiration during a summer of great adversity. The movie's themes of success and overcoming hardships were messages I needed to hear during that season.

Like Ritchie Valens, the main character of the movie, I was in a new city. I had to leave family, friends and plans behind. Despite my younger siblings' belief that this trip was about an athletic summer camp, I knew it was also related to our parent's relationship challenges. Their fifty-year marriage had its ups and downs like every marriage, but the summer of 1987 was when they worked things out.

On that balcony, my mind wandered. I thought about how my life would have turned out differently if I had stayed behind at home. I questioned my mother's decision to bring us to Los Angeles and wondered if there were other options for our family.

Abruptly, I was quickly rescued from the past pain when I noticed a pair of beautiful twin palm trees illuminated by the rising sun. The picturesque sight of those trees towering over Westwood Village popped out like a 3-D image over a backdrop of pink and golden skies. As I watched the palms blowing in the wind, I marveled at the beauty of life and the goodness of God. The trees reminded me that even when life takes unexpected turns, what's on the horizon will always reveal a brighter and better future than our past (Psalm 121:1-2, Job 8:7).

When we stick close to God through tough times, He will always give us double what we've lost (Isaiah 61:7). Why? God wants us to be assured that no destruction can come to our lives more significant than His plan to redeem us.

The ancient Israelites would burn palm branches, like the ones I saw that day, and use the ashes as a sign of mourning. Job, when he lost everything covered himself in ashes. Some Israelites were known to put ashes on their heads as a sign of grief (Joshua 7:6). As described in the book of Isaiah, beauty for ashes represents God's redemptive power that is available to us as an exchange (Isaiah 61:3). Many trials will come our way. Out of the ashes, we can rely on God's power to exchange our hopelessness with hopefulness. God gives us beauty for ashes and joy for pain.

I decided at that moment on the balcony that I would not allow painful memories to rob me of the unexpected blessings from the summer of 1987. In order to move back to Michigan, a family took me into their home so that I could return to my former high school. I came back in time to attend singing camp and sports training. I also gained a bonus family and sister-friend for life!

Our experience making ends meet in L.A. instilled in me a resourcefulness I have passed on to my children. To this day, my adult children expect a thought-provoking activity at family gatherings that teaches them resilience. I learned that dreams have a price, but they are worth shooting for and are absolutely possible to reach.

It's amazing how God will give us a new horizon to focus on instead of our current challenges (Philippians 4:8). When roadblocks are directly in front of us, it's easy to get stuck in a moment. However, if you have the faith to look past them, God will show you the way through or around them. He will even show you how to obtain double what you've lost.

When trouble arises, I always remember that it's darkest right before dawn. Breakthroughs come by remaining steadfast during life's storms. Don't let your heart be troubled. God is your advocate, and He will fight for you and return to you anything that has been lost or stolen (Exodus 14:14, Joel 2:25).

Definition (Meaning) of Horizon:

Dreams, opportunities, adventurers, wholeness

Prayer Before You Act:

Lord, thank you for giving me double back what has been robbed, depleted, or circumvented. Help me focus on what God is and receive your grace daily. I praise you in advance for complete and total restoration as you renew my thoughts, heal me from my past, and reveal the future you have for me. Amen.

Action Step:

Claim a double portion for anything the enemy has stolen from you and your family. As an act of faith, write out on the left side of your journal one to three things that have prevented you from trusting God. On the opposite side, write out what you feel the double portion looks like for you and your family. Identify one step you can take in the next seven days to realize your blessing.

BARNYARDS

DAY FOURTEEN

The LORD will command the blessing on you in your barns
and in all that you undertake. And he will bless you
in the land that the LORD your God is giving you.
~ Deuteronomy 28:8 (ESV)

In the Midwest, where I'm from, you are sure to pass a farm if you drive along the highway long enough. At some point, there will be a stretch of road where cornfields, crops, and cattle are ever-present atop perfectly manicured fields.

During a family trip, I noticed something I had never seen before, five large barns spread across a particular property. Farmhouses usually have a shed, equipment, animal life, and only one barn nearby. This one had five. A few of the barns were old and rundown. Others looked brand new. One even appeared to be built out of cheaper materials and lacked the structural integrity of the older ones. They were clearly built for a purpose.

The farmers worked hard all year and were expecting an abundant harvest (Genesis 2:15). They built additional barns to hold everything they expected to reap. No matter how things turned out, the farmers remained diligent to sow and reap year after year (Genesis 8:22).

As my view of the farm transitioned to my rear-view mirror, I began to wonder whether or not I'd be ready if a great harvest suddenly appeared in my life. Would there be space for me to incorporate and cultivate those seeds I had planted? Did I have enough room to receive what I'd been asking God for? Could my calm demeanor lead to unpreparedness and a delayed harvest (2 Corinthians 2:11)? Would I miss out on what God had for me because I wasn't paying attention?

In times of drought, it's easy to feel like the harvest will never come. But we must catch our thoughts and encourage ourselves when everything seems to have dried up (1 Samuel 30:6, 2 Corinthians 10:5). All abundant harvests require seasons of sowing, tilling, and watering. If you stay faithful to the promises of God and continue to work your land, you will receive all that God has promised. Whether you can see the seed growing or not, He is faithful (Hebrews 10:36). Knowing God's will is simpler than you might realize. There are six ways the Bible shows us how to align ourselves with God's will:

1. God's will brings peace (Colossians 3:15, Isaiah 55:12, Romans 15:33).

2. God's will never violates the written word of God (Psalm 138:2, Psalm 119:05).

3. God's will does not violate love (1 John 4:8, Leviticus 19:17, 1 Corinthians 13).

4. God's will requires faith (Psalm 84:11, 2 Corinthians 5:17 and 5:21, Psalm 145:19, Proverbs 10:24).

5. God's will requires us to seek counsel (Proverbs 11:14, Proverbs 18:1).

6. The desire for His will grows as we seek Him and dwell in His presence (Psalm 37:4).

When we actively align ourselves with God's will we walk the path of abundance—a life of overflowing harvests. That's the journey of trusting God, living with His understanding, and following His direction. However, when we lower our expectations, we are like a farmer who doesn't expect a harvest.

Maybe life has taken you from a shout to a whisper. Perhaps you've been taught to equate humility and meekness with mediocrity and timidness. Maybe you've experienced so much drought that you've forgotten what an abundant life looks like.

I have good news for you today! He has not forgotten your prayers. God has destined you and has set you up to reap a great harvest (1 Peter 2:9)! It's finally time to expand your mindset and begin to believe for the abundant harvest. Heaven is working right now on your behalf. Even though you can't see it yet, the good seeds you have planted have taken root. It's time to build barns and prepare for the harvest.

A good farmer knows when the seeds they have planted will grow and bloom. They even use a Farmer's Almanac for insight about long-range weather forecasts and to predict the harvest time. Like a good farmer, God knows the precise schedule of when our harvest will appear. He never fails.

Even when we don't know the timing of our breakthrough, we should watch our crops with expectation and pray over them earnestly (Psalm 5:3). In other words, you must remain vigilant during every season. Why? Unlike seasonal fruit, God's promises can be harvested at any time or in any season (2 Timothy 4:2).

Today it's time to expand your capacity for the harvest you have been expecting. Your harvest is beyond your wildest dreams (Ephesians 3:20). It will fill your barns to the brim. It will overflow more than you could ever ask or think! That means whatever is coming will bring provision for generations to come. It's time to build your barns!

Definition of Harvest:

The process or period of gathering crops (bring in, reap, collect, pick).

Prayer Before You Act:

Dear Lord, I know you planned great things for my life. Thank you for blessing me to cultivate the seeds you have planted and those that have already sprouted. As I wait in expectation, I pray for the strength to continue tilling the land you have given me. When the barns are full, help take care of my harvest. Amen.

Action Step:

Write out three seeds you have planted and the harvest you expect them to produce. Make three titles for the seeds you believe will sprout and fill your barns. Once you create your list of titles for the seeds, document the growth process. Describe what *has* been produced under each seed title, no matter how small. Finally, write down one simple step you can do in the next seven days to water your seeds and help them grow.

CLIFF JUMPER

DAY FIFTEEN

Be strong. Take courage. Don't be intimidated. Don't give them a second thought because God, your God, is striding ahead of you. He's right there with you. He won't let you down; he won't leave you.
~ Deuteronomy 31:6 (MSG)

There was a time when I was hyper-focused on improving my life. Despite my best efforts, things were still unstable. My children were at the age where everything Marcus and I did was challenged. Our business was experiencing growing pains, and I still had doubts about my purpose outside of marriage and motherhood.

Feeling stuck, I began asking God to provide direction, but I only heard crickets. Despite my best efforts, there were no answers from on high. Regardless, I was sure that over time He would tell me which way to go (Jeremiah 42:3).

I knew that my faith and family were at the top of my priority list. However, we also needed the finances to meet our basic needs and fund our dreams. I was so thankful we had been blessed with a great provider, protector, and leader in Marcus. At the same time, I needed to prioritize my time and create a better lifestyle for our family.

For a period of time, all my "brilliant" ideas only seemed to complicate matters. I finally realized I had to surrender, relax, and truly believe God was in control (James 4:10). I would not find the answers through guts, grind, and grit. Instead, I needed to wait on the Lord and believe He would direct my path.

I have visited Jamaica many times over the years. Many thrill-seeking tourists would visit to watch adrenaline junkies jump off the gigantic cliffs and plunge into the water below. Each time I visited, I became more curious about this dangerous sport.

One day, I had my opportunity. While attending a wedding, our newlywed friends chartered a boat to the cove near the same cliffs. Once we were anchored, our tour guides gave the passengers time to cliff jump. I don't know what sparked inside me, but I actually considered it. Yes, I enjoyed watching others jump, but I wanted to experience the thrill for myself.

Instantly, my heart began beating rapidly. I realized that it wasn't the jump I was leery of. I was terrified of landing in deep, dark waters (Matthew 6:33-34). Back home, I had been stuck, unable to fully jump into the life I wanted. I had struggled to put my trust in God and in my own abilities.

I knew I had to stop doubting and make a leap of faith. Would I keep watching others leap and go get the life I wanted? Was I ready to trust God, follow His purpose, and courageously jump into His promises? It would start with that symbolic leap into the sea.

Scripture tells us that God will always open a door that no man can shut. However, it is still up to us to walk through the door and refuse to fear what is on the other side (Revelation 3:7).

As I prepared my mind for the cliff jump, I diligently waited my turn. When our guide came to escort the last group, I thought about what this jump meant for me personally. Fear gripped me for months, and this was my chance to push through. I quickly grabbed a life jacket and climbed up the platform. As I looked down below, I vowed to myself never to let fear stop my purpose again (2 Timothy 1:7).

During my ascent, I passed multiple people who, at first, bravely climbed the steps. Now, they cowardly held onto the cliff walls. Once they had a closer view of the drop, they hesitated. Many turned around and returned to the boat. As I watched others retreat, I had to fight the urge to do the same. The fear in their eyes tempted me to run. Regardless, I knew I could not go back. This was a breakthrough moment. God had prepared for me to conquer this challenge.

When you are on your "purpose path," you must guard yourself against what others may fear or think. Progress requires focus, regardless of the distractions surrounding you (Psalm 119:37). It also requires the courage to think for yourself.

I am proud to say I faced my fear that day and jumped from that platform. When I broke the surface of the water, I could see the beautiful coral-covered ocean floor. Only those brave enough to jump could see this scenery.

Not long after we returned to the states, I stumbled across a documentary about the dangers of cliff-jumping. I had no idea that it was classified as a "deadly thrill-seeking activity." The narrator explained that hitting the water at a high rate of velocity could result in injury or death.

A last-second hesitation from pre-jumping jitters could cause a jumper to slip and hit the side of the cliff before reaching the water. There are also hidden dangers like rocks under the surface.

The associated risks with my cliff jump confirmed the meaning of my breakthrough moment. Something profoundly changed within me as I leaped from the platform and entered the ocean. As I emerged from the Caribbean Sea, I felt empowered to move forward. I could overcome anything.

If God said it, all I had to do was jump using my God-given courage. He would protect me (Ephesians 1:19-20). It was as if the illusion of fear washed off and remained in the sea. It taught me that no matter how high you climb, how far you jump, or how unsteady circumstances might be, God is with me (Isaiah 43:). He will never leave me even when Heaven seems silent. I realized that being brave means pressing through circumstances despite feeling fear. Your reward will outweigh any temporary discomfort (1 Peter 5:10).

Definition of Brave:

Ready to face and endure danger or pain, showing courage. To endure or face—unpleasant conditions or behavior—without showing fear.

Prayer Before You Act:

Dear Lord, You have given me the courage to walk through my challenges. I know you are near, and I will choose to trust you always. Thank you for strengthening me. No matter how big or small the door may be—or what surprises await behind them—I believe that you have empowered me to walk through them. When I am weak, I am made strong in you. Amen.

Action Step:

How has fear hindered your progress? Write down your fears, including the reasons or excuses behind them. Did your fears ever take place? If not, what would your life look like if you took a leap of faith and begin again?

This exercise is designed to help you to recognize that divinely assigned opportunities will continue to show up in your life until you jump. Do not give in to the pre-jumping jitters. Step onto the platform and GO GET YOUR LIFE!

DON'T SNOOZE

DAY SIXTEEN

Lord, in the morning you will hear my voice;
In the morning I will pray to you, and I will watch for your answer.
~ Psalm 5:3 (ISV)

In the wee hours of the morning, I reached for my alarm clock to push the snooze button for the second time. Despite my best efforts to beat the sun and work on my book, I was developing a terrible habit of hitting the snooze button multiple times each morning.

It was true that both Marcus and I were overextended and overwhelmed. Between building a business, directing a non-profit, raising children, and other commitments, I was exhausted. Some days the snooze button flat-out won the battle. I grew so frustrated with my newfound tendency that I moved our bedroom clock across the room.

One particular morning after the alarm blared, I got up, walked across the room, and hit the button. Once back in bed, I knew something was different. I couldn't get comfortable enough to fall back asleep. I could feel time literally escaping from me. The harder I tried to doze off, the more restless I became.

Then, without warning, I heard a booming inner voice say to me, "Get up! Be careful! You are snoozing your life away!"

"Wow!" I thought, "Now that was a wake-up call!" Quickly, I got out of bed and went to work. The following day I did the same thing. Instead of hitting the snooze button, I woke up, jumped out of bed, and seized the day.

Pausing the alarm clock every few moments and hoping to extend our sleep can seem like it's providing us with more rest. In reality, it's not. Why? Snooze sleep is not the vital REM sleep our body needs. REM sleep is where we dream, process emotions, develop the brain, and consolidate memory. It's where our wakefulness preparation takes place.

Hitting the snooze button can also rob us of the morning. Science shows that we are more mentally alert in the morning rather than at night. The morning is also an ideal time to pray and meditate (Psalm 63:1). It's a valuable time to seek God, receive instruction for the day, and find clarity for our goals.

Like hitting the snooze button in the morning, you can also hit snooze on your dreams. It was the great Pastor Noel Jones who said, "Procrastination is the enemy of time and results in lost opportunity." The habit of procrastination, like my habit of hitting that snooze button, can slowly steal our future. In our adult years, my father would repeatedly tell us, "You think you have more time than you do, but you don't." As I've become more mature and awakened to the things of God, I know that to be absolutely true.

Make the decision today to quit pushing life's snooze buttons. Olympic skier Lindsey Vonn once said, "Follow your dreams. If you have a goal, and you want to achieve it, then work hard and do everything you can to get there, and one day it will come true." When you're working toward your dreams, know that dreams won't create themselves. They need your perseverance and the wisdom of God. If you are willing to rise up early and welcome the Holy Spirit, I guarantee He will reveal Himself to you and do more than you could ever imagine (Psalm 25:14, Ephesians 3:20)!

Definition of Snooze:
A short, light sleep, especially during the day.

Prayer Before You Act:
Father, I thank you for helping me to remain diligent in finishing the plans you have for me. When I feel weary, thank you for the strength to keep walking toward my promises. With your help, I will overcome any obstacle. Give me proper natural rest as I lie down and supernatural rest as I trust in you. With your strength, I won't snooze through life (Psalm 18:29, Jeremiah 32:17).

Action Step:
Set your clock earlier than usual by at least 60 minutes. If you have a hard time waking up early, subtract an hour of sleep to extend your day at night. Do this for the next seven days, especially on the weekends when we purposely sleep in.

Dedicate this single hour to developing a personal project. It could even be one you've pulled off the shelf or birthed out of an action step initiated by this forty-day devotional. After the first week, repeat as frequently as needed. Add this action step to your daily schedule.

Note: I encourage you to apply this action step in the morning, even if you are not an early riser. Try it for a few days. You might like it.

RUNNERS TAKE YOUR MARK!

DAY SEVENTEEN

*You've all been to the stadium and seen the athletes race. Everyone
runs; one wins. Run to win. All good athletes train hard. They do
it for a gold medal that tarnishes and fades. You're after one that's
gold eternally. I don't know about you, but I'm running hard for the
finish line. I'm giving it everything I've got. No lazy living for me!
I'm staying alert and in top condition. I'm not going to get caught
napping, telling everyone else all about it, and then missing out myself.*
~ 1 Corinthians 9:24-27 (MSG)

I always look forward to hitting the ground running on the first day of
the new year. Regardless of how late we celebrate the night before, I wake
up early and review my resolutions.

A few years ago, I experienced a nagging hesitation. As much as I wanted
to plan out my future, I realized that my resolutions might actually be
hindering my progress. I put too much pressure on myself. I would
regularly set unrealistic dates to accomplish specific goals. That meant
that even though I finished most projects, I still had tasks I was not able
to finish.

"This year," I told myself, "my strategy had to be different." Instead of planning my whole year, I would begin by finishing incomplete tasks from last year. As I reviewed what was still left to do, I felt overwhelmed.

Despite my humongous to-do list, I remembered that God was orchestrating my steps (Deuteronomy 1:30). Although I felt stuck, I also knew I needed to change my perspective. I needed to focus on completing my current tasks with excellence, be patient with myself, and trust in God. If I did, I would lay a foundation for myself to achieve more success in the future.

Purposeful starts are vital for any runner who intends to win. Before a runner begins a race, they hear the command, "On Your Mark, Get Set, Go!" A great runner knows that setting their feet and body in the proper position before they sprint can be the difference between winning and losing. That's why runners regularly practice the art of the standing start.

What is true for runners is also true in life. If you want to set yourself up for success, you must put yourself in the proper starting position. Like Olympic runners, take the time to prepare for the race. Steady yourself by standing on the promises of God (Hebrews 6:18). Although it might require you to pause, you will be adequately equipped to run your race. You will move forward confidently and forget the past behind you (Philippians 3:13).

God has placed you on your "mark," so you might get "set" and ready to "go!" Just remember the things God has whispered to you. He will train you, equip you, and partner with you. Therefore, be patient and get ready! At any moment, the sound of the starting pistol will be heard (James 1:4)!

DEFINITION of "On Your Mark, Get Set, Go!":

A three-command start when racing: on your mark (get on your lane), get set (get in your lane or spot), go (take off)!

Prayer Before You Act:

Dear Heavenly Father, I ask you to expose the desires of my heart that have fallen by the wayside. I am open to your instructions to begin again and finish what I started. I will be intentional with how I set myself up before I go forward. Set me on my mark and steady my approach. Amen.

Action Step:

Do you have any incomplete resolutions from last year? Choose one and complete it before moving on to other tasks. God will give you the strength to finish it.

TAP ROOTS

DAY EIGHTEEN

Let your roots grow down into him and
draw up nourishment from him.
See that you go on growing in the Lord,
and become strong and vigorous
in the truth you were taught. Let your lives overflow with joy
and thanksgiving for all he has done.
~ Colossians 2:7 (MSG)

There was a season in my life when our family received tragic news month after month. We experienced death, hospitalizations, mental health emergencies, and a devastating false accusation that threatened our children, finances, and freedom.

Trials and tribulations bombarded our lives in rapid fire. I pleaded with the Lord to make it stop. It didn't. It continued for several months. A series of events caused extended family ties to crumble in a way that only God could heal.

Although the season felt unfair, I knew in my heart that other families were facing far worse circumstances. This helped me remain hopeful. Still, I begged for relief. I stood on my faith, believing that God would deliver us, expose the enemy, and bring restoration to our lives.

Despite our circumstances, I continued to press forward in the best way possible. I continued to teach "The CALL" (Caring About the Lives of Ladies - Now Go Get Your Life, with Coach Charese) on Facebook to encourage other women and coach my FAT (Fit Accountability Team). During this tumultuous time, I began having my daily devotional time outdoors to get some fresh air, peace, and quiet. Spending time in nature daily had a transformational effect on my mindset and mood during that season.

Then one weekend, it rained heavily in Michigan. The runoff was so terrible that it caused enough flood damage to summon FEMA to our local area. After the rain had stopped, I got up extra early to have coffee and prayer at sunrise. When daylight began to illuminate the yard, I noticed a massive clearing in the foliage. This was unusual because the nature preserves behind our home are filled with trees that legally cannot be removed. Puzzled, I looked closer and found a giant root stem from a fallen tree. "It must have been uprooted by the storm!" I thought to myself.

The root stem was massive. Originally, I was thankful the tree had fallen in the opposite direction and avoided our home. Secondly, I had no idea a storm had the power to pull the tree's root system out from the ground. I was fascinated.

I couldn't help but incorporate the exposed root into that season. With each rainfall, the ground around the tree's roots softened. Furthermore, the tree was on a slope. Even though the tap root, the main root, was anchored, the fibrous, the supporting root system, was not grounded enough to hold the tree in place.

Marcus and I felt like that tree. The storms in my life had worn us down as a family. Would we be able to withstand the rain without sinking, sliding, or falling over? I had to put my trust in God to stay steady. I'd have to know that He'd bring me out of this stormy season. After all, our family, business, and everything we held dear was ultimately rooted and grounded in Him (Proverbs 11:8).

Unlike the tree in our yard, with God, the anchor of our root system, there was no way we could fall. Instead, we were like the tree described in Jeremiah as one planted by springs of living water. Every season—even in drought—we would still bear the fruit of the spirit that lived within us (Jeremiah 17:7-8).

After that fateful morning, I had confidence that God would see us through. He had made promises to our family, and I knew He would not break them. He couldn't (Hebrews 6:18). Whatever the weather would throw at us, we would make it through. Our roots went deep in God.

Romans 8:31 says, "When God is for you, who can stand against you?" When your roots are grounded in the Lord, you can weather any storm (1 John 5:4-5). Despite the trials you find yourself in, thank God in advance that He is with you and will see you through. Walk confidently and know that He answers your prayers.

If one thing is true, it's that there are many storms in life. It is also true that while storms will always pass, God stays the same. Even though we are hard-pressed on every side, we are never crushed (2 Corinthians 4:8-9). No matter how many rain storms come, the sun always breaks through every rain cloud. Meanwhile, find shelter in God (Proverbs 8:10). Keep your hope in Him, and you will never be disappointed. Let Him be your anchor, and you will never be uprooted (Hebrews 6:19).

Definition of Taproot and Fibrous Root:

Tap root: a primary root that grows vertically downward and gives off small lateral roots. The central element or position in a line of growth or development.

Fibrous root: A root (as in most grasses) that has no prominent central axis and that branches in all directions.

Prayer Before You Act:

Heavenly Father, thank you for the opportunities to grow deeper in you. Thank you for helping me to become rooted and grounded in you so that I might have the strength to withstand any storm. I believe you will keep me from sliding or falling even when things are falling down around me. May every storm I face teach me how strong I am in you. Amen.

Action Step:

There are several types of root systems. Of the two mentioned above, which one more closely describes your relationship with God during this season? If you have been on a slippery slope that has caused you to drift away from God, what can you do to level it out before you slide or fall? Strengthen your root system by spending time with God and trusting His promises.

THE PLAN IS STILL THE PLAN

DAY NINETEEN

And we know that all things work together for good to them that love God, to them who are called according to his purpose.
~ Romans 8:28 (KJV)

Years ago, I was part of a marketing company that included a wellness division. We promoted healthy habits, accountability, and the importance of nutritional supplementation. I joined a fitness challenge sponsored by that company to push me through the final stretch of a weight loss battle I had been fighting for many years.

I would be competing against hundreds of contestants from around the world but I knew I could place in the top 20%. After the first few weeks of competing, I realized I had a chance at winning the cash prize of $50,000! My children were growing up and becoming more self-sufficient. I had more time to concentrate on daily workouts, food prep, and supplementation.

Then, one afternoon I received a call that would change our lives forever. I was asked to take temporary custody of a three-year-old. If I declined, the little girl would be removed from her home by CPS immediately. Petrified by the anguish I heard in this mother's voice, I immediately said, "Yes!"

By no fault of her own, she had been catapulted into our lives. Taking in a foster child was taxing (John 15:13). We weren't prepared to deal with the state's checklist, parental visits, checkups, and daily care.

To make matters worse, behavioral issues caused conflicts at school that often interrupted our work days. I got used to expecting a call from the school office at any given moment asking me to pick her up for the remainder of the day.

Over time I could see my energy was running low. I was burning the candle at both ends of the stick, trying to stay in the winner's circle of the competition. I was just about to submit my final "after" photos and stats on deadline day when the school called with yet another behavioral breakdown. They needed me to come right away.

I hesitated. I wondered if I had the time to pick her up and make it back home in time to upload the proof of my transformation. I could not abandon my commitment to stand in the gap for this little girl (Psalm 10:14).

As she and I walked to the car after a long meeting with the principal, I checked the time and realized I could still make it. Once I got home, I began to upload my 'before and after' photos in a hurry. As I watched the computer clock count down towards the deadline, the cut-off passed before my files had completely uploaded.

I was devastated. I questioned my judgment in thinking I could foster parent when it seemed we were already stretching to manage what we had on our plates. I also pondered how the prize money could have helped our family and thought about how much time and energy people like my trainer Gary Wade had invested in me. As I reviewed the results of my competitors, it became clear that I had achieved the most significant physical transformation. I knew in my heart that I had just let $50,000 and a chance to expand my weight loss coaching slip away.

The next few days were rough. I felt extremely depressed and resentful toward myself. I ignored calls from my trainer, my father, and my friends. I began to sleep in longer and eat more to soothe my negative feelings. When I did talk to people, their attempts at encouraging me with clichés like "everything happens for a reason" didn't help because I felt that the reason was me!

While the children were at school, I lay in bed for several days in broad daylight. Unable to lift my heavy head from the pillow, I continued to ask God why and how this could have happened. Suddenly, something came to mind. *"All* things work together for the good of those who love the Lord and are called according to His purposes" (Romans 8:28). At that moment, I knew I would be OK even though it would still take time to get over the disappointment.

A few weeks later, I received a call from the vice president of the company, who was also the director of the weight loss division. To my surprise, he invited me to speak at the upcoming convention. My transformation was so notable it was recognized by the corporate officers despite my disqualification. They wanted to showcase my transformation.

Due to the depression I was feeling, I had stopped training and eating clean for the last few weeks. However, the phone call was enough encouragement to snap me out of mourning and return to the gym. Romans 8:28 had clicked! I could see things beginning to work together for my good.

I learned a valuable *"yesson,"* which is a yes that brings about the unforeseen but teaches a great lesson. While setbacks and letdowns can be painful, you never know how God will manifest your breakthrough.

As Tim Storey often says, "Instead of letting your setback make you take a step back, get ready for your comeback." In my case, I almost let the loss of the competition reverse my fitness transformation and overshadow the opportunity our family had to pour into this little girl's life (Philippians 4:8).

It was a test that would eventually become a huge part of my testimony and ignite my purpose. When I experienced the true power of Romans 8:28, I made it my life's mission to empower others to go get their life regardless of the setbacks they endure. As I learned how to help others lose weight, both in pounds and emotional heaviness, I was given the name "Coach Charese." Since then, that name has stuck with me as I've continued pursuing my passion. God turned one of the most challenging seasons of my life around and made it work for me. This season inspired me to help others reach their goals. *That* was the true prize and ultimate promotion. I owe all of it to the Father, who never ceases to amaze me! Never forget that God's plans will come to pass even when they don't seem possible. If a door closes on an opportunity, He can open a window. God knows how to purposely make it all work together for our good, so we can walk in our purpose!

Definition of Opportunity:

A set of circumstances that makes it possible to do something. A chance, occasion, moment, opening, option, or window.

Prayer Before You Act:

God, I believe your plans for me are yes and amen. Your promises are always true. As I do my best to walk out my purpose, I thank you for keeping me on track and working everything out for my good. Help me to avoid missteps along the way with your guidance and provide me with the assistance of every angel available to me in Heaven and on Earth! Amen.

Action Step:

Can you think of a time when things seemed to be going in the wrong direction, and they suddenly turned around? Was it a time when something that seemed impossible suddenly became possible? Take a few moments and write down what happened in your journal and how it can encourage you today.

Give an example of what seemed impossible.

1. How did this situation turn around for your good?

2. What are you currently hoping will turn around in your life right now?

SEEDS OF PURPOSE

DAY TWENTY

"I cry out to God Most High, to God who fulfills his purpose for me."
~ Psalm 57:2 (ESV)

While on a long walk one day, I listened to the audio version of Rick Warren's best-selling book, *The Purpose Driven Life*. The book outlines God's five key purposes for His people. When it concluded, I meditated on purpose. If God has given each person a unique purpose, then why wasn't it easier to define for so many?

It had been years since I had listened to Warren's words. During the early 80s, many retired professional athletes, including my father, toured the speaking circuit. As guest speakers, they promoted authors like Rick Warren and Dale Carnegie, who preached on finding your purpose.

When I was eight years old, I would listen through the crack of my father's office door as he practiced his speeches. My mother was also a big promoter of self-motivation and encouraged us to believe we could do great things. She was also extremely driven. My mom completed several marathons and almost trained for the first women's Olympic marathon in 1984.

Our mother believed in the power of mind over matter. From a young age, she taught us to memorize mantras like "you can do it if you put your mind to it" and "what the mind can conceive, the body can achieve." As children, my siblings and I wholeheartedly bought in. At the time, we believed all things were possible (Mark 9:23-24). But as we grew older, that belief became challenged by the hardships of life.

No matter how far we have strayed from our childhood dreams, I believe we will always be drawn to our purpose. Our seeds of purpose have already been planted inside of us, just waiting to be watered (1 Corinthians 3:6-8). When we delight ourselves in Him, we receive a clear revelation of our unique purpose path that God has already sown in the desires of our hearts (Psalm 37:4).

We are all born with a purpose to discover. Sadly, there are so many people who still struggle to find it. Some fear that they never will. Blindsides and roadblocks show up that often interfere with fulfilling our purpose. If God has promised to give us the desire of our hearts when we delight in Him, why do we sometimes struggle with finding what has been predetermined?

I am reminded of a friend who struggled to foster his natural gifts because it didn't seem that they would financially support his family. Still, his passion for art continued to call to him as he got older. Rather than ignore his inner desires, he practiced daily in his bedroom. Then, one day he had the opportunity to lead the creative design team for one of the most iconic theme parks in the world. His story is a simple yet powerful reminder of what happens when we water the seeds God has planted within us.

Today, my friend is a world-renowned artist. He discovered his purpose by sticking to his passion and watering his seeds. His work is showcased worldwide; he is now considered a master of his craft.

God has given us the gift of life and divine purpose. It's our assignment to fulfill every purpose He has for us (Psalm 57:2). When we know our purpose is divinely inspired; we can walk confidently. Regardless of what we've been through, we can still find our way back to purpose at any age. Be patient. In life, there is a time and season for everything. Seeds of purpose take time to bloom, just like natural seeds before a great harvest. Take the time to water your purpose seeds every day and trust God that he will bring the increase at the right time.

If you feel like you struggle to find purpose, have no worries. You can cast your cares on God and give Him your ashes. Why? Because he will exchange those ashes for a crown of beauty. As we find the joy of the Lord even in our mourning, I believe anything can be restored (Isaiah 61:3)! Today, trust in the Lord. Give him your dead things and let Him give you new seeds. If you stay true to watering them every day, the increase will come in a mighty way.

Definition of Germinate:
To grow or to develop. When a tiny seedling cracks through a seed casing and sprouts, it has germinated

Prayer Before You Act:
Lord, I believe you have stored seeds of purpose for my life inside of my heart. Thank you for helping me identify and nurture those seeds I have tucked away because of circumstances. Thank you for bringing an increase to areas needing new life. Regardless of my past decisions, or the challenges I now face, let the desire to fulfill your purpose grow in my heart. I put my trust in you because you created me to have a purpose-driven life. Amen.

Action Step:
Are there seeds in your life that are planted in unhealthy soil or near weeds? It may be time to prune, uproot, and transplant old seeds for new ones.

Identify one to three seeds in your heart.

1. Reflect on why they are not growing.

2. What is one step you can take toward a solution?

3. Plan a time to water your seeds.

OH, WE HAVE PLACES TO GO!

DAY TWENTY-ONE

But those who wait for Yahweh's grace
will experience divine strength.
They will rise up on soaring wings and fly like eagles,
run their race without growing weary,
and walk through life without giving up.
~ Isaiah 40:31 (TPT)

Have you ever received a promise from the Lord—maybe through a prophecy or during your devotional time—that remained unanswered when you needed it the most? One morning, during my devotional time, I began to lose patience for a promise I had been waiting on for a very long time. I had become so consumed with *how* it would happen that it felt better to give up on the promise all together.

At the time, I was still a young business owner in my twenties. I was in debt, newly married, and a new mom. My responsibilities weighed heavily on me as I fought worry and indecision. I struggled to stand firm (1 Corinthians 16:13).

Despite the anxiety I felt, I was at a crossroads. I could give in to my worry, or I could wait on the Lord and use this as an opportunity to grow spiritually (Isaiah 40:31). Besides, I knew that God's promises were true.

By intentionally choosing to wait on the Lord, I began to AIM my wait toward His promises. I chose to be Active, Intentional, and Mindful of the waiting season. As I AIMed, I became energized rather than weighted down. Instead of feeling defeated, I felt charged up and full of faith! I soon discovered that AIMing my wait made me more productive and less idle. As I increased my productivity, I began to see glimpses of God's fulfillment of His promises (Proverbs 19:15). The more I saw, the less I worried and the more I was encouraged.

In his last book, *Oh, The Places You'll Go!*, Dr. Seuss tells the story of many people who get stuck in "the waiting place." It's a place where people can spend their whole existence waiting to begin their life. I believe people get stuck in "the waiting place" because they have not learned how to AIM their wait properly.

When we find ourselves waiting on God's promises, it's easy to become complacent. If we don't AIM our wait, we can become fearful, cynical, and resentful (Proverbs 16:27). When that happens, we can let our waiting rob us of great things to come. This is why it's essential to AIM your wait, so you don't lose heart.

I believe God allows us to wait on promises to teach us the power of AIMing our wait. To AIM is to know that God is working behind the scenes on your behalf. It's to live with hope for the future and be open to what heaven has said. God uses your waiting to prepare you for what He has promised (Hebrews 3:4).

Contrary to Dr. Seuss, I believe "the waiting place" can be a valuable space meant to prepare, equip, and align you with what God wants to give you. The choice is yours. You can waste your wait or AIM your wait.

If you can learn to AIM, you'll be able to reach the places you *were* meant to go without wavering, wandering, wondering, or worrying.

Coach Charese's Definition of A.I.M.: (Actively, Intentionally, Mindfully)

- **Active:** positive, energetic, or vigorous way. Intentional preparation.

- **Intentional:** deliberately; on purpose. A clear purpose, intentional action, and a clear purpose and focus.

- **Mindful:** attentive; heedful: careful. State of being conscious or aware

Prayer Before You Act:

Lord, help me while I wait on You. Empower me to hold on to Your promises with hope. Help me to do the work using the power You placed inside of me. Help me to apply the Word to my situation while allowing You room to fill in the gaps. As I wait, help me not to grow weary or disheartened but instead encourage myself as I stand firmly on your promises. Help me to wait as you prepare me to receive more than I could ever ask or imagine. Amen.

Action Step:

Can you identify one life goal or spiritual promise—that you've been working toward or believing for—that could benefit from better AIM? Write out your promise or goal and one step you can take actively, intentionally, and mindfully.

THE ICE BATH: "SHOCK, SHIFT, AND SETTLE"

DAY TWENTY-TWO

"Are you tired? Worn out? Burned out on religion? Come to me. Get away with me and you'll recover your life. I'll show you how to take a real rest. Walk with me and work with me—watch how I do it. Learn the unforced rhythms of grace. I won't lay anything heavy or ill-fitting on you. Keep company with me and you'll learn to live freely and lightly."
~ Matthew 11:28-30 (MSG)

When I played sports, I only witnessed two reactions when athletes plunged into an ice bath. They would either slowly settle into the ice bath or jump out as quickly as possible. Why? When the 50°F ice water hits your skin, nerve endings send messages to your brain that trigger a fight or flight response.

Ice baths have been a part of naturopathic alternatives to medicine since the 19th century. Although ice baths are therapeutic and beneficial for health, the shock from the cold water makes it difficult to believe they are actually good for you. Professional athletes use ice baths to recover quickly from minimal injuries.

There have been times in my life when I felt like God placed me in a spiritual ice bath designed to shock, shift, settle and restore me. This especially happened when I was sidetracked by distracting commitments.

Growing up in a house of nine children had its ups and downs. The upside to being raised responsibly meant I learned to be strong, independent, and resourceful. The downside has been that I have the tendency to help others at the expense of my own needs.

Several years ago, I assisted a traveling minister whose armor bearer had recently married. My initial intention was to assist her during ministry assignments for a few weeks. As I began to serve, I quickly found that the schedule of meetings started to grow. On top of those ministry assignments and my overextended personal life, the prayer calls, revivals, and conferences multiplied. Before I knew it, a few hours on a Sunday morning turned into all-day commitments.

Many days I became the traveling pastor's driver. Although the role was never defined, it eventually became expected. Those few weeks of extending my help turned into two years. Eventually, I became tired, overworked, and weary (Galatians 6:9).

Even though I was sure she could find a replacement, I never told tell her how I felt. Instead, I stayed stuck in "help mode" like young Charese. Rather than slow down, I put my head down and continued plowing. Somewhere along the way, I had been programmed to think that it is better to put the needs of others before my own.

Like athletes who plunge into ice baths, my life was about to experience a shock. The more I ignored my feelings of exhaustion, the more deficiencies appeared in our home, our businesses, and my body. The work of the ministry began to feel more like "works." My weariness meant I had no time to invest in my visions and dreams. Areas of my life that used to produce fruit—my professional and social life—dried up.

The moment arrived when my life came to a standstill. While driving to a ministry engagement, my truck began to shutter and clunk. By the time I got home that night, it had cut off and would not start. After further inspection, it turned out I needed a new engine. It would take several weeks for the mechanics to order and install the parts. During that time, everything stopped. I could not attend ministry meetings, run errands, or go into the office.

The engine breakdown had led to a dramatic life shift. Like an ice bath, it shocked me into submission. Finally, I realized the mistake I had made. I had not been obedient to the dreams God had given me for my life and my family (Galatians 5:16). I had taken a significant detour. While well-intentioned, I had sacrificed my purpose path for the purpose of someone else's.

It's easy to get sidetracked when you're in service to a good cause. The lives impacted by the ministry kept me engaged in serving, giving, and sacrificing. However, there is a difference between what needs to be done and what you should be doing. We all have unique responsibilities according to our purpose in the kingdom of God. When we take on a commitment that is not our own, we will often sacrifice our real purpose in the process.

Sometimes we must be shocked into changing direction for the sake of our calling. However, just like an ice bath, the shock can be good for you. I can still remember how inconvenient it was to manage an active household and run our businesses with one vehicle. At the same time, less responsibility ultimately led my spirit to be renewed and my focus to be restored.

Like the ice bath, these life shifts can bring healing, restoration, and clarity. It's amazing how God loves us so much that He will shock us into shifting our lives (1 Corinthians 10:13).

79

When we don't take care of ourselves, we limit our ability to help others. When we stay on our own purpose path and practice self-care, we set ourselves up to be agents of God's purpose for those around us (Isaiah 58:12). Only when we are restored can we become His hands and feet in the world.

Definition of Jolt:

Push or shake (someone or something) abruptly and roughly; an abrupt movement.

Prayer Before You Act:

Dear God, You have blessed me to be a blessing to others. Please help me know who, what, when, where, and how to assist those who need help. Show me how to obey you better. Sharpen my discernment when sacrificing my time, talent, and treasure. Amen.

Action Step:

Do you have an open-ended commitment that sidetrack you from accomplishing your goals and dreams? It could be taking care of someone, a recurring professional obligation, or even an extra-curricular activity. Take a few moments to write down how different your life would be without those extra commitments and what simple steps you can take to relinquish those responsibilities.

SELF CONTROL

DAY TWENTY-THREE

His master said to him, Well done, you upright
(honorable, admirable) and faithful servant! You have
been faithful and trustworthy over a little;
I will put you in charge of much. Enter into and share the joy
(the delight, the blessedness) which your master enjoys.
~ Matthew 25:23-24 (AMPC)

For many years, I struggled to get my weight under control. During most of that time, I failed to deal with my inner issues that kept my weight in a constant state of flux. I knew I had the discipline to follow a weight loss program successfully and had done so many times. In fact, my mother even put me on Weight Watchers as one of my first diets at eleven-years-old. I'm confident my parents had the best intentions to help me manage my weight. However, in between those diet regiments, I developed the terrible habit of binge eating to cope with insecurity. As my weight increased, I became more insecure. In turn, I would cycle between binging and gaining more weight, then purging and dieting.

As I got older, I could only keep the weight off when disciplined enough to stick to training and strict diets. But once I reached a physical goal, the weight would always come back. Then, one day, after decades of yo-yo-ing, it clicked. If I was going to keep the weight off, I had to do more than rely on my grit and grind. Instead, I needed to practice a lifestyle of self-control.

Self-control is what sustains long-term change. If you can foster self-control, you can overcome short-term impulses and bad habits for good (Luke 8:13). Like an auto-pilot system, self-control can override the urge to eat the pizza your family ordered and enforce the discipline to eat salmon instead.

Discipline is driven by our sheer will, while self-control is a fruit of the spirit. We receive this from God through time spent with Him. In order to conquer obesity, I would need self-control in addition to discipline.

You see, discipline is the ability to repeat specific actions to produce the results we want to see. It's the habits and behaviors we stick with to improve. Self-control, however, is the ability to reject specific behaviors that hinder our progress. It's the power to stop and remove the behaviors that weaken us.

Self-control is a pre-request to discipline. By refusing to do the things that weaken us, we create room for behaviors that makes us stronger. Self-control also comes from within. I knew how to perform the steps that led to weight loss, and I was great at seasonal discipline. But due to my deep insecurities, I did not have the self-control to stop using food as a coping mechanism, like an unhealthy seed that produces unhealthy fruit. If I was going to develop self-control, I had to sow healthy seeds that would blossom into the lasting self-worth I needed to transform my life.

This simple revelation changed everything. When I approached the challenge spiritually, I noticed the first few weeks were not as overwhelming as they had been in the past (Matthew 11:30). Once I understood the root cause of my unhealthy eating habits and how to address them, I felt I could finally lose weight and keep it off. Equipped with a new mindset, I set out on my weight loss journey once again.

As I lost weight this time, I noticed an inner confidence I had not felt before. Instead of feeling emotionally crushed when I would fall short of my weekly goals, I felt patience and self-love. When I was tired, I heard an inner voice reminding me to keep going. I now believed that I was valuable and worth it.

As I reached my ideal weight, I didn't feel like a new me. Instead, I felt my inner voice say, "Finally, I'm really me!" My outer weight had been reflecting my inner self-worth. Reaching this internal, personal milestone made it much easier to maintain a healthy weight. It was the turning point that ignited my journey to dedicate my life to helping others realize their self-worth and reach their dreams.

No matter who you are, where you are, or where you come from, you can walk in the abundant life you desire through the power of self-control (John 10:10). We grow self-control when we are willing to uproot personal beliefs that produce bad fruit and plant new seeds that will create a great harvest.

It doesn't take much to plant good seeds. I tell my clients that only a small dose of self-control is needed to completely transform an area of their life. This is true because practicing self-control only leads to more self-control. The Book of Proverbs says that the Lord establishes our steps (Proverbs 16:9). When we apply what the Lord teaches us in scripture, our steps become established. God is going to build on what we are willing to do. He takes the self-control we perform and multiplies it.

Remember, an apple on a tree is still an apple, even if it is small. Just give the fruit a chance to grow, and it will remain. Before you know it, you will have elevated your life in ways you never thought possible (Matthew 25:23). This is why you must always remain rooted and grounded by faith (Matthew 17:20). Water your seeds of faith with His Word (Isaiah 58:11). Speak His Word over your life through positive affirmations (Philippians 4:8). Finally, practice discipline until the fruit of self-control appears (James 1:4, Isaiah 40:31).

Self-control is one of the most important fruits of the Spirit because it helps you resist temptation when you've been called to greatness. It also correlates with how the other eight fruits of the Spirit show up in our lives. We will need self-control to show **love** to the unlovable (Luke 6:27), experience **joy** amid sorrow (Nehemiah 8:10), have **peace** in every situation (John 14:27), demonstrate **patience** when we are being pressed (Romans 12:12), extend **kindness** after unkind interactions (Ephesians 4:32), provide **goodness** when things aren't so good (Matthew 5:44), practice **faithfulness** and remain loyalty when others have failed us (Hebrews 11:1), and show **gentleness** in a harsh world (2 Timothy 2:24-25).

Anything worth doing requires overcoming adversity. Refrain from being surprised when you meet opposition. Remember, you are breaking habits and dismantling beliefs that had to be uprooted, transplanted, and watered with the Word and positive affirmation.

God wants you to have every fruit of the Spirit as evidence that you are walking with Him. If you abide in God, your life will be full of fruit. Like a blossoming tree, you will have all the self-control you need to become the person God created you to be. Today, take heart, sow good seeds in your life, and water them. If you do, you will see a harvest of self-control.

Definition of Self Control:

The ability to regulate one's emotions, thoughts, and behavior in the face of temptations and impulses. As an executive function, it is a cognitive process necessary for regulating one's behavior to achieve specific goals.

Prayer Before You Act:

Today, I take responsibility for my actions toward stalling progress in any life area. As I increase my self-control, I thank God for your daily grace and mercy in applying the discipline needed to see the increase. I thank you for every fruit of the Spirit available to make me the best I can be, live a balanced life, and walk in abundance. Amen!

Action Step:

There are specific ways to grow self-control. Some include knowing your strengths and weaknesses, removing temptations, setting goals with plans to execute them, and becoming more diligent. Think of a simple task that you can't seem to complete due to lack of self-control.

1. If you have started and stopped moving forward to completion, what are the things that caused you to stop?

2. Did you set a specific plan to execute them?

3. Did you implement any form of accountability? If so, what were some of the reasons the accountability failed?

4. Do you have a positive talk track around what you want to accomplish with self-control?

5. Have you forgiven yourself for not completing this goal?

Note: Enlist a trusted coach or accountability partner. Forgive yourself quickly and move on if you waiver.

DIESEL FUEL

DAY TWENTY-FOUR

You make known to me the path of life; you will fill me with joy
in your presence, with eternal pleasures at your right hand.
~ Psalm 16:11 (NIV)

Have you ever wondered why the diesel nozzle is larger than the one used to pump regular gas? This was a question I thought about after stopping to fill up my tank and mistakenly attempting to place the diesel nozzle into my SUV.

One dad, when I needed gas for my car, I had accidentally grabbed the diesel nozzle. After realizing my mistake, I was extremely relieved when the pump did not fit into my gas filler. If not for the irregular-sized nozzle, that small mistake would have caused significant problems. It would have damaged the engine and hindered my vehicle's performance.

Due to its differences from gasoline, diesel full requires a different engine. Diesel is a fuel derived from oil with a thicker state of fluidity than gasoline. It also packs in more energy. It is not as combustible and does not burn as quickly as traditional gasoline.

After my mishap, I discovered I wasn't the only one who tried to fill my gas-powered car with diesel fuel. It's a common mistake many people make despite the extreme difficulty of fitting a diesel pump nozzle into a typical gasoline filler. In fact, the gasoline neck and the diesel fuel nozzle are purposely designed to be incompatible. Still, some people manage to pump diesel fuel into their gas tanks and ruin their engines.

When cross-contamination occurs, diesel fuel severely affects a gas-powered vehicle's health. What is true for car engines is also true in life. Allowing contaminants in or around prosperous areas of our lives can cause interference and long-term damage. The faster we become aware of our mistakes, the less our time, talent, and treasure will be damaged.

Unfortunately, in life, we don't always have clear differentiators, like on the diesel nozzle, to stop us from filling ourselves with the wrong things. This can be especially true in times when our spiritual and emotional tanks are running low. Taking time to assess our surroundings and checking our "tank" levels is crucial to our progress. Only pump things into our lives and bodies that empower us rather than break us down.

In the Bible, oil is a symbol of spiritual vigilance. Throughout scripture, oil often represents the Holy Spirit, whereas anointing symbolizes the Lord's favor. This is why we need to intentionally stop at the "filling station" and check in with God, who provides the oil. Prayer gives us the pit-stop we need to fill us up and keep us in motion. When we pray regularly, we guard ourselves against burnout and breakdowns.

Oil is precious. Steer clear of people who siphon your fuel (1 Corinthians 15:33). Everyone is not fueled up with the right gas to take the journey with you (Proverbs 13:20). As the great Booker T. Washington once said, "Associate yourself with people of good quality, for it is better to be alone than in bad company."

Even though gas and diesel are derived from crude oil, they fuel different types of engines. God anoints everyone for a specific purpose. He always gives us exactly what we need and strengthens us to carry any load. We receive our unique anointing when we spend time with Him (Proverbs 20:24).

Our purpose is sealed, but it's God's oil (anointing) that we need to unlock it (2 Corinthians 1:21-22). This anointing will teach us the truths we need to know and prepare us as we stay on our purpose path and united with Him (1 John 2:20, 1 John 2:27).

Every day, spend time with God at His and keep your tank full. It can sometimes seem inconvenient to stop and pull over for gas, but it's certainly better than running out. What is true for cars is true for prayer. Take the time to pray, and you'll always have enough to manage whatever is in front of you (2 Timothy:1-2).

Take a moment and reflect on how far you've already come. You have made it through things you could never imagine—sometimes while running on fumes. When the gas light comes on or you feel a chug in the engine performance, pull over to fill up with prayer and God's Word. If you do, you will always have the energy to finish strong and the power to make it over any mountain.

Definition of Diesel:
Awesome or strong, as in physical power.

Prayer Before You Act:
Dear God, Help me to recognize the things that prosper your perfect plan for my life. Clearly and swiftly expose anything that takes me off my purpose path. As I spend time talking with you, I trust you will fill me with the energy and power I need to reach my final destination. Thank you for your anointing. Like oil, Your Spirit keeps my engine running smoothly and full steam ahead. Amen.

Action Step:

What do you have in place to block anything that threatens to slow or stop your forward movement? Is there anything in your life that does not fit into your current season or your future? It may be something that has been around for a long time. If it has the potential to contaminate your oil (spiritual vigilance and preparedness), find a way to clean it out before any long-term damage can occur.

GPS: GOD'S PURPOSE SIGNAL

DAY TWENTY-FIVE

"Set up signposts to mark your trip home. Get a good map. Study the road conditions. The road out is the road back. Come back, dear virgin Israel, come back to your hometowns. How long will you flit here and there, indecisive? How long before you make up your fickle mind? God will create a new thing in this land: A transformed woman will embrace the transforming God!"
~ Jeremiah 31:21-22 (MSG)

Before the days of GPS or Google maps, the only options for navigation were to travel by memory, write out turn-by-turn directions, or follow a road map. I'd often travel by memory to places I had been before. My favorite way of staying on the route was to use landmarks and confirm I was moving in the right direction. I remember a few times when landmarks I relied on were changed or removed. When that happened, I became concerned about whether I'd gone the right way. As I continued to drive, my surroundings looked familiar enough to keep going.

Nevertheless, I'd hear a small inner voice questioning whether I was going the right way. Sometimes I would listen to that voice and second-guess myself. It led me to turn around or become lost.

Through modern navigation tools, there is a new voice that guides me, the voice of my GPS. Since I bought my first smartphone, I have always made it to my destination.

It's easy to second-guess life decisions, especially when traveling through unfamiliar territory. Being unsure if you're making the right decisions or headed in the right direction is universal to the human experience. That's why it's essential to pay attention to God's principles and tune into His GPS (God's Purpose Signal). If you do, you'll never get stuck driving in circles. Instead, you'll always know the right path.

According to lyrics.com, at least 140,873 lyrics in the history of songwriting mention going round and round. That's a lot of singing about driving in circles.

On any given day, the average person can make up to 35,000 decisions and spend roughly sixty minutes questioning them. If we carefully consider each decision's outcome beforehand, we can reduce the amount of time spent in regret. I found this to be true in my own life. I have spent as much time thinking about completing my to-do list as it would have taken to complete it. What is true for finishing a chore is also true spiritually. When we focus on what God has said about us, we don't have to question our self-worth. We can walk boldly and confidently forward as His children and complete our God-given assignments.

It's amazing how God's grace always meets us where we are at. Even when we are stuck spinning our wheels, He nudges us. He provides guidance using the Holy Spirit as a Global Positioning System. It's up to us to listen for those directions and follow them (Isaiah 29:24). When we have gone too far or lost the signal, know that it's OK to stop and ask for help (Psalm 121:2).

It's important for movers and shakers to stop and look at a situation before proceeding. We have to learn to "stop, look, and listen," as Tim Storey says. He has used this practical phrase to help many people move forward and avoid setbacks en route to their God-given calling.

The Biblical story of the Exodus is the account of 600,000 Israelites' journey out of Egypt toward the promised land. Before they reached their final destination, they spent forty years wandering the desert. During those years, many died in the wilderness because they struggled to follow God's Purpose Signal (GPS). They instead worshiped false idols. As a result, they missed the new land filled with milk and honey that God wanted them to possess.

Many people get stuck in their setbacks and are unable to experience a comeback. Like the Israelites, they wandered the desert for years, missing opportunities that could change their situation. Out of all the initial 600,000 Israelites that left Israel, only Joshua and Caleb survived. They believed in and followed God's Purpose Signal (GPS), which directed them to possess the promised land.

Despite the rough terrain and giants, they had faith in God's Purpose Signal (GPS). In doing so, they made it through the desert and possessed the land promised to them. The story of Joshua and Caleb perfectly shows the power of following God's Purpose Signal (GPS) and the dangers of ignoring it. It is to our advantage to diligently follow His instructions when navigating through life. Don't go at it alone or stick to the easy path. God has a tailored set of plans for us stored in His GPS. It's a direct route through the rough terrain and will take you through the fulfillment of your purpose (Isaiah 45:2-12).

Definition of Destination:
The place to which someone or something is going or being sent.

Definition of Road Map:

A plan or strategy intended to achieve a particular goal; A detailed plan to guide progress toward a goal; A detailed explanation.

Prayer Before You Act:

Lord, help me to surrender to your perfect plan for my life. Thank you for your grace guiding me so that I stay on track for the abundant life you promised me. En route to my promise land, thank you for provision especially when I encounter giants and detours. Throughout this journey, I pray that I remain committed to my relationship with you. You are doing new things in and around me. Help me receive what is specifically meant for me, no matter what others say or do. You are my Shepherd, and I shall not want as you lead me beside still waters and restore my soul. Your goodness and mercy shall follow me all the days of my life (Psalm 23:1-6)! Amen.

Action Step:

Scope out your land (your life) and allow the Holy Spirit to show you where you may not be following God's Purpose Signal (GPS). With that in mind, address the following...

1. Is there anything you've intended to do that you've been circling around?

2. Write down any concerns that are causing indecisiveness.

3. How would your life be positively affected if you stopped circling and completed it?

4. What directions are being given by GPS (God's Purpose Signal) right now that you can follow?

BIRD BOX

DAY TWENTY-SIX

This is what I told them: 'Obey me, and I will be your God,
and you will be my people. Do everything as I say, and all will
be well!' 24 "But my people would not listen to me. They kept
doing whatever they wanted, following the stubborn desires of
their evil hearts. They went backward instead of forward.
~ Jeremiah 7:23-24 (NLT)

When the world closed down during the pandemic, my grown children were home. Every day we looked for ways to spend time together doing activities we could all enjoy. During our Netflix nights, I noticed many of the most popular movies streaming paralleled the times we were living through. One of these films, *Bird Box*, is the story of a woman named Malorie Hayes. She is played by Sandra Bullock, who is trying to protect herself and her two children from a mysterious force that decimates the population. Even though the film never reveals what the entities look like, whoever looks at them dies.

Malorie and her children have many close calls throughout the film. With each encounter with an entity, Malorie discovers more about them. Eventually, she realizes that birds become frantic when close to an entity, so she captures a few for security. Armed with only her inner voice, birds in a box, and her will to live, Malorie overcomes all odds and saves her children.

The story serves as a profound metaphor for the power of believing in oneself and staying true to the inner voice. Like Malorie kept her eyes shut tight no matter the danger around her; we, too, must resist giving in to our greatest fears.

The Bible calls Satan the Father of lies. He attempts to draw us away from our purpose through fear (Philippians 3:13). We must never stop listening to the inner voice that calls us forward and gives us the courage to push through—our intuition. In those moments when we cannot be led by our eyes and ears. Intuition is not enough. We need to be led by the Spirit. He orders our steps. His Word is a lamp for our feet in a dark place (Psalm 119:105).

I couldn't help but think of how this movie symbolized what many people felt during the pandemic. The world changed so rapidly that many people closed their eyes or "bird boxed" in the face of uncertainty. Some of the strongest, most faith-filled people became overwhelmed by the news reports. Looming danger and economic uncertainty hung over the world like a dark cloud. A simple errand like going to the grocery store required courage to mask up and face the threat of infection. If you were not careful, you could become frozen in fear.

In those moments, it was crucial to follow the inner voice. That inner voice is a divine gift from God (John 16:13). Intuition gives us the confidence to move forward, especially when we struggle to make our way through the storm. God has given us the ability to hear Him, so we can navigate away from trouble. It's that same voice that also helps us find our treasures. We can rest knowing that no matter what tries to pull us away from our promise, we have our own helper who's better than any bird in a box (John 14:15-21).

People often ask me how to hear and know the voice of God. I tell them there are layers to hearing and knowing God's voice. The first key is to get to know

Him. The simplest way to get to know the Lord is to read His Word and learn the heart of God. It is the foundation for a great relationship with Him.

The second key is knowing that God's voice transcends natural intuition. This happens through perceiving. To perceive means to become conscious or aware of something by sensing it through God instead of our natural senses. For example, while the Apostle Paul was on trial after being arrested in Acts 27:10, he expressed, "Sirs, I *perceive* that this voyage will be with hurt and much and much damage, not only of the lading (cargo) and ship, but also of our lives." Before it happened Paul received revelation from God about the future of the ship and its crew.

The third way God speaks to us is through prompting. We are led when we feel a gentle nudge or something crosses our mind. It's like having fleeting thoughts that lead you to act. The nudge can come from an immediate desire to call or check on someone. It can also be a desire to pray over someone in church.

Finally, God can speak through us through a check in our Spirit. A check can show up through feelings of uneasiness or loss of peace. It's when we know that something isn't right or that something is wrong. We know this is not fear because it comes from within. Fear is brought on by external factors and not by God.

When we choose to listen to the voice of God, especially in times of trial, we can walk confidently and know God is leading us. The more we give ourselves over to that confidence, the louder His voice becomes. The more we delight ourselves in Him, the sooner He grants us the desires of our hearts. These desires God has for us were placed in our hearts at the foundation of the Earth (Psalm 37:4, Philippians 2:13).

Ultimately, Malorie and her children found safety in a school for the blind. By learning how to thrive using their other senses, they were never deceived again. As they depended on their sense of touch and hearing, the fear of the mysterious entities became powerless over them.

During the covid-19 pandemic, it was difficult to look at and accept the realities of our times. Whether we wanted to look or not, it was happening. We might have sometimes felt like crawling under a rock and hiding while the world became a different place. In unsteady times, it's easy to be tempted to entertain unhealthy outlets that take our minds off things.

There have definitely been moments in my life when I wished I could put on a blindfold. However, in life, there are some things we must face. Be encouraged during these seasons because we have help. Let us never forget how we can hear and know the voice of God. Let it always be our guide, even when we do not want to look at what lies ahead.

Definition of "Turn a Blind Eye":

Overlook; Disregard; Neglect; Ignore. Pretend not to notice.

Prayer Before You Act:

Dear God, thank you that I can hear and know your voice. I am confident you will guide me and order my steps with your Biblical truth. Thank you for the strength to face any problem before me. With your assistance, I have no need to fear. You are my eyes when I cannot see or am too scared to look. I will trust you to deliver me from anything that causes me pain. Amen.

Action Step:

I believe God holds the solution to every problem we could ever face and has given us access to the answer key. Although tests can be intimidating, God is faithful. Grab from your memory bank the most recent example of a time when it seemed easier to cover your eyes.

1. Describe briefly the situation you didn't want to look at.

2. Were you able to eventually face it?

3. Was there a prompting, a perception, or a check that helped you navigate through?

4. Is there a lesson you learned following God's voice (or not) that will help you face difficult situations in the future?

TARGET PRACTICE

DAY TWENTY-SEVEN

*I'm not saying that I have this all together, that I have it made.
But I am well on my way, reaching out for Christ, who has so
wondrously reached out for me. Friends, don't get me wrong:
By no means do I count myself an expert in all of this, but I've
got my eye on the goal, where God is beckoning us onward—
to Jesus. I'm off and running, and I'm not turning back.*
~ Philippians 3:12-14 (MSG)

I was asked to appear on a reality show for a family friend and support a client. The show was produced in Los Angeles. Anyone traveling from out of state at that time had to be quarantined before going on set. With little choice, I decided to take advantage of those three days of isolation by fasting and praying.

Before the trip, my prayer team was standing on God's Word for the healing of my friend's son, who had recently been hospitalized. I attempted to connect with my friend at her house and at the hospital before I left town, but I was a few minutes shy of catching her. As the week progressed, the situation became more critical. The night before my trip, I set an early alarm, so I could swing by the hospital en route to the airport. As the alarm went off the following morning, I hit the snooze button twice. My late-night packing session had left me more tired than I had anticipated.

Once I boarded the plane, I sent an apology text to my friend because I could not stop by the hospital before my flight. I also told her that I was standing in faith with her for her son's full recovery. I promised her I would visit when I returned.

After landing and taking my phone out of airplane mode, I discovered an urgent text. As I read her message, my stomach sank with regret for snoozing rather than keeping my word. It was a plea asking me to pray fervently and contact every prayer warrior I knew. I, along with her close friends and family rallying around her, needed to bombard heaven. They needed a miracle!

Sadly, later that night, I was informed of her son's passing. In disbelief, I immediately began to feel a groaning in my Spirit for my friend. I thought about how she had supported me when one of my children wrestled with debilitating health challenges. She had been there for me, but I was unable to reciprocate. Though I knew there was nothing I could do now, 2000 miles away, I also knew I had missed a window to serve.

The more I thought about my friend's grief, the more I became emotionally overwhelmed. My feelings eventually turned into tears. For the next three nights, I'd wake up in the middle of the night crying. The more I processed my mistake, the more I grieved for her loss.

During those few days, I managed to return a few calls from concerned mutual friends. One call was from one of my closest friends, who I will refer to as Ayn. Ayn was someone I spoke to daily. She is also someone I have known for almost my entire life. Knowing me so well, she knew this experience would most likely trigger emotions I felt from losing my little sister. As she inquired about how I felt, I had no real answer. I was still trying to figure that out.

As we discussed what had happened, she continued to press. All of a sudden, it hit me like a tidal wave. All the memories of times I thought I'd failed others came rushing back. The regret I felt in those moments turned into self-condemnation. I knew I was beating myself up unfairly. As Ayn and I continued our conversation, I broke, began to weep, and blurted out, "I missed it! I just missed it!"

Then a loud thought interrupted everything. I knew it was the voice of the Holy Spirit jumping in to comfort me (John 14:26). He said to me, "You won't always hit the bullseye placed before you. When you are off the mark, God's grace will fill the gap and make the crooked places straight (Isaiah 45:2)." At that moment, I had to accept my own weakness and limitations while also accepting the unlimited grace of God.

The lesson God was teaching me in that hotel room was clear. In life, we sometimes miss the mark. Despite our best efforts to be perfect, we fall short. Despite our desire to control every situation, sometimes all we can do is surrender. The guilt I felt had to be exchanged for self-love. It was a powerful revelation that forever changed my perspective on perfection and guilt.

Sometimes life can feel like target practice. It's important to remember that the shots we miss are not made in vain. Failure is how we grow. In fact, it will increase our accuracy for the next marker set before us. Never forget to aim with sincerity and good intentions. Continue to press toward the mark. When you do, you still might miss your mark on the first try. However, over time, you will always find yourself right on target.

Definition of Press:

Move or cause to move into a position of contact with something by exerting continuous physical force.

Prayer Before You Act:

Dear God, as I work on accomplishing my goals, I need your help adjusting my aim to hit the target. Help me hear your voice clearly so I can walk confidently forward. When I miss the mark and fall short, help me to remember that your grace is sufficient and there is no condemnation in You. Thank you for giving me multiple chances to hit the marks you've placed before me. I appreciate the grace that covers my shortcomings as I aim. Amen.

Action Step:

Is there a target you are aiming at but find yourself struggling to hit the bullseye? Maybe it's your fitness goals, career progression, or just taking time for yourself. Take a few moments to assess your form and strategy. Are you stable when shooting toward the goal? Are there any distractions blocking your view that can be removed? Are you aiming toward the target using a well-thought-out plan that can get you there?

If you answered no to any of the above questions, take a few more moments and jot down the adjustments you need to make to hit the target. If the target has passed (like an enrollment period for school), that's OK. Complete the exercise with that target in mind, and you'll be ready when the mark appears again.

THERE IS NO WIZARD, AND THIS IS NOT OZ

DAY TWENTY-EIGHT

"...but thanks be to God, who gives us the victory
[as conquerors] through our Lord Jesus Christ.
Therefore, my beloved brothers and sisters,
be steadfast, immovable, always excelling in the work of the Lord
[always doing your best and doing more than is needed],
being continually aware that your labor [even to
the point of exhaustion] in the Lord is not futile
nor wasted [it is never without purpose]."
~ 1 Corinthians 15:57-58 (AMP)

Growing up, I was always excited when the classic film *The Wizard of Oz* appeared on television. My mother would lay out a blanket in front of the oversized white console that encompassed our bubble television. Then, she would serve us popcorn mixed with M&Ms or Fiddle Faddle. As we watched, we anticipated when the colorful characters would come on screen. We all could recite the Wicked Witch of the West's iconic line "I'll get you my pretty!" on cue.

At that age, I did not realize how many life lessons were embedded in my favorite childhood film until I watched it as an adult with my own children. Although the movie discusses themes that might seem scary for a young person, the lighthearted singing and dancing woven between the challenges kept me believing Dorothy would make it home.

The story begins when a Kansas tornado blows Dorothy and her house to the magical land of Oz. Upon receiving directions from the Lollipop Guild, she begins her journey to receive help from the Wizard of Oz by following the yellow brick road. Initially, the road appears to be bright and shiny. However, as she travels farther, the path becomes dark, and the trees become narrower with every step. Along the way, Dorothy stumbles upon a great big lion, a squeaky tin man, and a lovable scarecrow, who are all clearly struggling along their own paths.

At each stage of her particular journey, Dorothy must face her fears. As her bravery grows, she becomes a force of encouragement in the lives of her new friends. By the movie's end, Dorothy encounters a talking forest, a poppy field, flying monkeys, and evil spells. Every time, she overcomes her challenges, pushes through with positivity, and increases her determination to find her way home (James 1:2).

The film comes to its conclusion when Dorothy reaches the magical city of Oz and the Wizard. To her dismay, the great Oz lacks the power to assist her. Severely disappointed, Dorothy gathers herself and heads toward the exit. Before leaving, her dog Toto pulls back a curtain, revealing a fearful old man—the real Wizard. It turns out Dorothy never needed to locate the Wizard of Oz or click her heels together three times to return home. Dorothy had what she needed inside herself all along.

The story is a profound lesson in the power of encouragement. Many times in life we have to encourage ourselves, especially when we're the lead cheerleader for others (1 Samuel 30:6). That's why it's so important to speak words of life over ourselves (Proverbs 18:21). In Dorothy's case, her words of life came in the form of songs.

It is also important to surround yourself with good company who have the desire to discover and fulfill their purpose as well, rather than those who are idle (1 Corinthians 15:33). Through every challenge, Dorothy sings cheerfully with her companions. When she feels frightened, the lyrics redirect her thoughts and give her the courage when she feels afraid.

What is true for Dorothy is also true in our devotional life. Philippians 4:13 says, "I can do all things through Christ who strengthens me." Whenever I believe I'm called to do something difficult, this is my go-to scripture. This verse shows up in the "Go Get Your Life!" devotional multiple times because it's an excellent scripture to have in your arsenal. If you declare it over yourself, it will remind you that you are strong enough to do anything! Your confidence comes from God, who gives you the strength to complete whatever you set your mind to (Hebrews 13:6).

Dorothy discovered who she was by hearing what the lion, the tin man, and the scarecrow said about her. For us, we can find out who we are by hearing what God has said about us. There is nothing greater than the power of God that heals us and makes us whole. His truth sets us free when we understand our identity in Christ. There is power at work in us, and we have to reach the point where we trust in God's faithfulness (Ephesians 3:20).

There's a story in the Bible about a lame beggar who sat outside the Beautiful Gate in Jerusalem. Every day, he would ask people for money. One day a disciple of Jesus named Peter walked by. Instead of offering him silver and gold, Peter offers him healing and strength through faith in Jesus. The man's faith, combined with Peter's faith, gave the crippled man the strength to stand and walk. Many people witnessed what happened and were encouraged.

In Oz, the citizens went to the gates to see the Wizard daily. They, too, begged for him to help them, but Dorothy's faith, encouraged by Glinda, the good witch, set her free from the nightmare she had been in. In life, remember to always have someone you trust standing in faith with you while you're believing for your dreams (Matthew 18:19-20).

Whatever we face, go through, and come out of will never be wasted because God will always use it for our good and His glory. If we remain steadfast through it, those around us will be changed too. The people, who witnessed the miracle of the lame man, rejoiced. They believed they could be free from bondage. This also happened in Oz. Everyone who saw and heard of Dorothy's safe journey home to Kansas rejoiced. After that, they were never threatened by the Wicked Witch or the fraudulent Wizard of Oz again.

The Wizard of Oz became so famous that an urban version of the musical called *The Wiz* was produced. Instead of classic Broadway show tunes, *The Wiz* featured jazz and funk musical numbers. The movie's most famous song, "Ease on Down the Road," encourages audience members to journey down the path of life without fear and jettison any unnecessary weights.

Life can be overwhelming, which is why we need to give our burdens to God and ease the journey (1 Peter 5:7). As the song says, "The road you're walking might be long sometimes, you just keep on stepping, and you'll be just fine!" No matter what, if we keep moving, we won't lose ground even when facing opposition.

We don't have to be scared when confronted by fearful situations. God does not put fear in us. In fact, He has given us His love to cover anything, the power to press past everything, and a sound mind to remain focused on the truth (2 Tim 1:7). Therefore, there is no need to fear what God has already overcome.

In the final scene of *The Wizard of Oz*, it is revealed that Dorothy has been asleep the whole time. She wakes up and immediately appreciates her life and those in it. Along her journey, she faced her fears, learned how brave and powerful she was, gained confidence, and became a leader to her friends. Her experience transforms her from a young girl into a woman of power. Today, like Dorothy, trust in yourself and lean on the Lord. If you do, you will discover that you're stronger than you think you are. God orders each of your steps.

Definition of Breakthrough:

A sudden, dramatic, and important discovery or development (advance, development, step in the right direction, discovery, find, improvement, progress, headway, advancement)

An instance of achieving success in a particular sphere or activity.

Prayer Before You Act:

God, thank you for making me an overcomer. You have given me the power to tread on serpents and scorpions and overcome the power of the enemy. Help me face those fears that have kept me from elevating my life. Reveal to me the hidden fears that still hold me back. Fill me with the courage and self-confidence I need to be victorious. Amen.

Action Step:

Is there something you have been afraid to do? You may be afraid to start a new business, begin a new relationship, or take a risk. Search your soul today and identify one item you have been hesitant to work on and boldly face it today. You have the power inside to overcome that fear. If you are afraid to speak in public, take a class. If you are afraid of water, consider enrolling in swimming lessons. If new relationships are hard to start, then enlisting a counselor may help you process the pain of past relationships. While you work on the solution to relieve yourself of that load, begin to recite 2 Timothy 1:7 daily and ask God for guidance.

RUBIK'S TO RUBIX

DAY TWENTY-NINE

The Lord says, "I will guide you along the best pathway for your life.
I will advise you and watch over you. Do not be like a senseless
horse or mule that needs a bit and bridle to keep it under control."
~ Psalm 32:8-10 (NLT)

I was never able to master the Rubik's cube. Whenever it seemed I had every little square in the correct position, I wound up confused even more. Some people I knew during the early 1980s—when this was one of the most popular games in America—became masters of the cube. I was clearly not one of them.

Once, out of frustration, I rearranged the colored stickers on each square to make it look like I had finally solved the great mystery. Despite the outward cubes appearing organized, everything was still wrong on the inside.

That's what problem-solving without God looks like. The outward appearance often covers what we still need to resolve inside. I've tried to solve things on my own before without first going to God for His instructions. The more I ignored counsel, the more my problems became complicated.

We all wish we could keep our lives neatly organized, just like a new Rubik's cube on the shelves at the store. However, our lives can become quite scrambled depending on the decisions we make. There is no way to restore or straighten out our complicated lives without God's help (Zechariah 9:12).

Even though our lives are far more complex than a Rubik's Cube, it's easy to get impatient with God when He takes longer than we'd prefer. It's true that God has the power to unscramble our lives in an instant. It's also true that God has given us the responsibility to resolve some areas of our lives. Yes, He can solve our problems with one "turn of the cube." Still, when we make several turns with Him, He gives us the wisdom and understanding to bring order to our chaos (Proverbs 4:5-9). We are then discipled by God through that process and can apply our wisdom to maintain order (Psalm 119:71).

I'm sure I wasn't the first to give up on this challenging toy. Only 5.8% of challengers have been able to figure it out. According to computer scientist Tom Rokicki, no two solutions have been the same for all of the 43 Quintillion possible configurations. This number is unfathomable, yet God has an infinite number of solutions to problems that seem complicated to us (Jeremiah 33:3).

God desires to "Rubix" our lives, which is an actual word, according to the urban dictionary. It means to turn something from a mess to perfection. No matter what chaos we or external forces have caused, God can help us solve any puzzle this life brings. He has every solution stored up for us and has provided a way of escape (1 Corinthians 10:13). Spending time in His Word, in worship, and in this devotional will show you the solutions to go get the life God intended for you.

There is no need to worry or fear. No matter how big or small the mess. No matter what needs revamping or straightening, God knows and cares. He guides and watches over you. He will always be there to advise you with solutions at every turn.

Definition of Solution:

A means of solving a problem or dealing with a difficult situation.

Prayer Before You Act:

Dear God, You know the challenges I have overcome, those I am dealing with right now and those I have yet to face. I trust you to help me find the solutions I need to work through. You have always designed a way of escape for me. You are faithful to deliver me from the circumstances and the snares, no matter how severe they may seem. I declare today that I have found peace and strength in knowing that you are my rear guard, fortress, and help in times of trouble. I have no need to worry. Thank you for advising and watching over me. Amen.

Action Step:

Are you dealing with anything that looks OK on the outside but is bothering you on the inside? What one change could you make to turn it around, make it better, or perfect it? It could be as simple as speaking life instead of complaining. It might be distancing yourself from relationships that continually scramble your organized life.

Write down what God speaks to you as you step out on faith. Remember, God has more solutions to your problems than the possible configurations of a Rubik's cube.

CAKE

DAY THIRTY

And we know that in all things God works for the good of those who love him, who have been called according to his purpose. For those God foreknew he also predestined to be conformed to the image of his son, that he might be the firstborn among many brothers and sisters.
~ Romans 8:28-29

My late mother-in-law, Juanita, was a fabulous cook from Macon, Georgia. She could throw down in the kitchen at any moment. She taught me that no matter how insignificant it may seem, a pinch of salt or a dash of cinnamon could significantly impact a dish. Every ingredient has a separate function, but they all work together to create the chef's desired taste.

Following a recipe is based on something cooked before and deemed acceptable to reproduce. We can trust that if we heed those instructions, we will produce the same outcome every time.

Like a good recipe, God shares instructions for our life because He knows what works well. He is omniscient, omnipotent, and omnipresent.

We must learn to trust Him and receive His divine wisdom in His perfect timing. Even when we cannot see clearly, God guides us through confusion. The Message translation of 1 Corinthians 13:12-13 expresses this very well.

> *"We don't yet see things clearly. We're squinting in a fog...*
> *but for right now, until that completeness, we have three*
> *things to do to lead us toward that consummation: trust*
> *God, hope unswervingly, love extravagantly."*
> ~ *1 Corinthians 13:12-13 MSG*

We must trust this verse, especially when we feel like we are missing ingredients. Although God may give us a glimpse of the recipe for our lives, we must be patient. We have to wait for the circumstances to line up, just like waiting for an oven to warm up. We must wait for success the same way one waits for a cake to rise. Like a cake that cools after exiting an oven, we must rest in his presence after being burned by the fires of life.

Sometimes we only know bits and pieces (1 Corinthians 13:9). But we know that all the ingredients will come together to create a masterpiece. That's the beauty of God's faithfulness. He takes every ingredient from past mistakes, regrets, wrong turns, hurts, and pains and makes them all work together for good (Romans 28:29-30). That's why it is essential to remember not only who you are *in* God but who you are *to* God! We all have a distinct purpose attached to our lives. No matter how the enemy tries to scramble the recipe or omit an ingredient, God continually works everything out for us.

We have been given a recipe for life, and God has plans to prosper us. Sometimes the wrong ingredients are added. Sometimes the timing is off. The recipe can become tainted when challenges arise (Jeremiah 29:11).

Regardless, we are promised a brighter future no matter where we come from or what we go through. We can actually have our cake and eat it too. When life gets hot like an oven and feels like a pressure cooker, every ingredient will work together.

That's the power of God's grace. Even when we are missing an ingredient, God knows just what to do to create a far better version of anything we could create. Refuse the urge to doctor up the recipe, trying to fix the unfixable. Scripture tells us that God is the author and finisher of our faith. He is the master chef who takes our lives and makes something spectacular.

There is a story in the Bible about a widow of Zarephath who only had enough flour and oil to make her and her son one final meal. Because she obeyed God and fed His prophet, Elijah, God provided food for the rest of her life (1 Kings 17:8-16). What is true for the widow is also true for us. God will always take the little we have and turn it into more than we could ever imagine. All we have to do is focus on loving Him, and He will love us right back (Romans 8:28).

Have you ever been told never to stomp on the kitchen floor while baking a cake? The structure of a half-baked cake is very delicate. Any disturbance— a loud noise to a drastic drop in temperature—can cause it to fall.

Likewise, life brings disturbances that hinder our progress. Nevertheless, God promises we will rise if we trust Him (Acts 3:6-8). God knows every hair on your head and is attentive to your every need. He won't miss even the smallest ingredient (Luke 12:7, Psalm 34:15).

We are His sons and daughters, and He will never give up on us. Have confidence in Him like the best chefs you know. He will complete you no matter how long it takes to prep, marinate, cook, and cool. You will be made complete and whole in Him (Philippians 1:6).

Definition of Instructions:

Detailed information telling how something should be done, operated, or assembled.

Prayer Before You Act:

Dear Heavenly Father, help me wait for your instructions and remove anything tainting the recipe for my life and purpose. As you set a table in the presence of my enemies, I trust that you are also preparing a feast of your goodness that will follow me all my days. No matter what ingredients you have to work with, I'm so grateful that you have plans to use them and turn me into your masterpiece. Amen.

Action Step:

Have you ever felt you lacked the ingredients needed to create the life you've always wanted? Think about a time when God took one of your weaknesses and made it into a strength. God uses lessons and experiences you didn't initially know were valuable to bless someone else.

NOW THAT'S DEEP

DAY THIRTY-ONE

All these blessings will come upon you and overtake you
if you pay attention to the voice of the Lord your God.
You will be blessed in the city, and you will be blessed in the field.
~ Deuteronomy 28:2-3 (AMP)

For years I was in and out of treatment after a load of salon furniture fell off of a delivery truck and injured my back. After the incident, I began experiencing excruciating pain throughout the day and night. Doctors discovered that I developed spondylolisthesis (a spinal disorder when a vertebra slips forward onto the bone below it), had shifted pelvis, and pinched a nerve. Nothing seemed to be working. Then, one day, my husband did some research and found that natural saltwater could be an effective remedy. Within days, we were on our way to Negril, Jamaica, so I could soak in the natural saltwater.

Seven Mile Beach is one of my favorite places to vacation. I have been there several times. However, I would have never considered traveling there solely to take daily, holistic dips in the ocean.

Every morning and every evening, we went to the beach to soak, and it was working. One of those mornings, we noticed a few people on paddle boards suddenly shift directions and frantically jump onto a nearby floating dock. They abandoned their boards to escape whatever created a huge, lurking shadow on the seafloor.

I noticed the dark, ominous shape moving closer to shore. Many swimmers quickly exited the water. As I made my way towards the growing crowd, the adrenaline kicked in and canceled out any lingering back pain. Without realizing it, I started running toward the crowd. Once I got there, I discovered that the creature was a humongous stingray. Apparently, we were in a section of the beach named Stingray Alley. After talking to a few locals on the beach, they confirmed they had never witnessed a stingray that large come so close to shore.

I quickly strapped my husband's GoPro to my head. The stingray was moving slowly along the shoreline, so I took a shortcut by swimming under the buoys. As I approached, the GoPro hit a buoy line and was knocked off the mount. Before the small camera could descend too deep, I caught it in a panic. Quickly I aimed it toward the stingray that had settled a few feet from me in the white sand. Daringly, I walked alongside it, still filming the whole time. This massive stingray was at least six feet across and twelve feet long—roughly the size of a minivan! As my adrenaline continued to pump, I shouted toward my husband repeatedly, "I'M DOING IT! I'M DOING IT!"

After capturing fantastic footage, I realized I was probably pushing my luck. The poisonous tail was long enough to zap me right where I stood. When I returned to shore, I began to shake as I sat down on the hot sand. "Did that just happen?" I thought to myself as people clapped and high-fived me. I was so excited until my husband walked over with the bad news.

When I grabbed the GoPro camera out of the water after knocking it off the mount, I accidentally flipped the camera. I only recorded the water bubbles from my arm flailing across the giant stingray. I was so disappointed. I had chased the stingray for fifteen minutes despite back pain and risking my life.

To make matters worse, people kept asking if they could see the video I shot. News of the legendary act had traveled. It was unheard of for a stingray of that size to come so close to shore. It was even rarer to film it.

The disappointment lingered for a few hours. I had to snap out of it and remember why I was there in the first place. The Holy Spirit spoke to me, and I heard Him say, "It's not that deep."

I have heard many people say, "It's not that deep," meaning it's not that serious. Psalms 42:7 says, *"Deep calls to deep."* The Psalmist is telling us that God's Spirit calls our spirit. God wants to speak to the deep places within us. He wants to commune with us, so we desire a deep relationship with Him.

When we are willing to go deep with God, we are given glimpses of His promises to us, just like I glimpsed a gigantic stingray under the water. As His promises begin to manifest, we must accept them even when we can't see them clearly (2 Corinthians 5:7). Sometimes, He will call you somewhere beyond the place you're familiar with. When God calls you to deeper waters, trust in His perfect timing.

Soaking in the healing waters of Jamaica, I could never have expected a giant stingray to appear in the Caribbean Sea. It's hard to imagine our big dreams coming to fruition and suddenly surfacing from the deep end. However, if we can be still and know that nothing can stop God, a breakthrough will surface when we least expect it. (Psalm 46:10)

On the last day of our trip, Marcus took me back to Stingray Alley. We sat outside all day relaxing and reminiscing on what we called "ray watch." It amazed us how nothing is impossible for God even when it appears far away (Jeremiah 32:27, Luke 1:37). All it takes is focus and the willingness to dive deep into Him. When we do, we find a God who wants to express His deep and unending love (Proverbs 4:23).

Definition of *Deep Calls to Deep*:

The Spirit of God reaching deep into the spirit of His children, bypassing all that which would impede the fellowship God so passionately desires to have with us.

Prayer Before You Act:

Dear God, thank you for your deep and endless love and amazing grace. Help me when I struggle with disappointment. Fill me with your goodness and show me your deep waters. Reveal to me Your heart, and I promise to reveal to You mine. Grant me the peace to rest in the wait and the discipline to remain faithful. Align my life with your will so that I might be an agent of Your purpose. Amen!

Action step:

Have you ever relinquished hope for a promise? After writing the promise down, take three to five minutes and release any disappointment related to it. Finally, ask God to open your heart so that you believe what you wrote down will come to pass.

HALLOTHANKSMAS

DAY THIRTY-TWO

*In every situation [no matter the circumstances], be
thankful and continually give thanks to God, for
this is the will of God for you in Christ Jesus.*
~ 1 Thessalonians 5:18

One Christmas Eve night, I had the idea of decorating our living space
with all the outside Christmas lights and animated displays. I thought
it would be fun for the children, who were still toddlers, to wake up to
a "Winter Wonderland." We laid out colorful lights from room to room
and covered them with fake snow to create a glistening effect. We created
a Christmas display in our living room with an animated reindeer and
angels.

Our kids got so excited on Christmas morning that Marcus and I decided
to make Winter Wonderland an annual Christmas tradition. Every year
our indoor Christmas display would get bigger and better. Eventually,
it got so big we developed a reputation in the neighborhood. Neighbors
would bring their kids over to see it, and local delivery people would ask
to peek inside when they dropped off packages.

As the years went on, Winter Wonderland became more of a burden than a blessing. With our children now in college, it did not create the same experience it once had. It wasn't worth the amount of work required.

One year, I ended Winter Wonderland. Quickly, my family responded with lots of questions. I was initially surprised at how much it seemed to matter to my adult children. They acted like Christmas had been canceled.

The following year I resumed the labor of love. This time, I decided to start setting up Winter Wonderland much earlier. Instead of waiting to get everything prepared right before Christmas, I would begin the process in October. That meant, as a family, we could experience Winter Wonderland for Christmas, Thanksgiving, and Halloween!

As I began to execute my plan, I caught myself focusing so much on decorating for HalloThanksMas that I didn't give much attention to the message of Thanksgiving. "This is how we try to follow God," I thought to myself. "We often skip over the gratitude—the thanksgiving part—and just focus on receiving His gifts—the Christmas part."

It's easy to get caught up in the consumer Christmas spirit. From Black Friday to Cyber Monday, we are taught that Christmas is mainly about gifts. There is a build-up of excitement around who will get what and wish lists will be fulfilled. We wonder for weeks what's under the tree in anticipation of receiving those gifts. If we're not careful, we can miss the opportunity to experience the joy that accompanies the holidays. We can become so distracted that we miss the rich lessons God desires to teach us.

We must learn to be still and focus on God's voice. When He orders our steps, He takes us farther and faster than we ever could (Psalms 46:10). God is omniscient and omnipotent, and He is faithful to His word (Psalm 115:3, Hebrews 10:23, Luke 1:37, James 1:17).

I have found repeatedly that trying to carry heavy loads on my own, like HalloThanksMas, never works out. It's much easier when we surrender to God's plan. The sovereignty of God is always at work. He is the author and finisher of our faith. He keeps us on track toward our divine destiny. We align ourselves with that destiny when we commit to the spiritual practice of thankfulness.

Every day find simple ways to stay grateful. Remain in thanksgiving while you wait for the manifestation of His promises. Continue to be grateful when you receive a harvest and when you wait for others. Take time to notice all God is doing for you as he guides you toward your incredible future (Proverbs 19:20). Rest assured that His plans for you are already set. So, GO GET YOUR LIFE! with grace, patience, and thanksgiving!

Definition of Thanksgiving:
An expression of gratitude, especially to God.

Prayer Before You Act:
God, I thank you for giving me the discipline, courage, and awareness to slow down in this fast-paced life. You have given me enough time to accomplish my assignments and digest the lessons I learn. Show me your ways. I trust you and thank you for every divine step you have ordained to lead me to my harvest of plenty. Amen.

Action Step:
It's never too late to thank God for everything He has given you. Can you recall something you powered through just to "get it done?" In doing so, did you miss an opportunity to be thankful? Take a few minutes and write down what you were grateful for.

REPAIR THE BREACH

DAY THIRTY-THREE

He heals the brokenhearted and binds up their wounds
[healing their pain and comforting their sorrow].
~ Psalm 147:3 (AMP)

Breaches can happen for many different reasons. They can come in the form of offenses, violations, and failures. A breach can be a divorce, the sudden death of a loved one, or the falling away of a close friend. If a breach lingers long enough, resentment and strife could plague your relationships.

Regardless of who or what caused the breach, forgiveness is always the answer. Why? Because as hard as it might be to forgive, the path of unforgiveness is worse. Over time, unforgiveness carries a heavy price. It will rob you of future happiness, joy, and opportunities and prevent you from moving forward (Deuteronomy 30:19).

If you can find the courage to forgive those who have wronged you, I promise it will be well worth it.

From the beginning of my friendship with my husband, he would always tell me, "Charese, you will have to empty out those buckets of pain you have been holding for too long. This way, you can walk around lighter and be pleasant. Don't waste your life building calluses from ignored pain in places that don't deserve your energy. The true you will shine through. Everyone will see who you truly are."

Something I personally struggled with for a long time was controlling my emotional responses toward my children, husband, friends and employees. I knew that my behavior was connected to past hurt that manifested when I was under pressure.

I have learned that holding onto the past won't change the person or situation that hurt you. In fact, if you hold on to it long enough, it can cripple you. Unchecked hurt can manifest in bad attitudes, snappy responses, impatience, and crotchety dispositions. It can create a toxic environment that can also infect those around you (Hebrews 12:15).

If you find yourself struggling with anger, bitterness, or resentment, Ephesians 4:31 is clear—the answer is forgiveness.

Forgiveness is a powerful spiritual gift that includes much more than saying a few words; it's an active process of letting go of negative feelings towards someone, whether they deserve it or not. It is the path from anger to praying for our enemies (Matthew 5:44). It's a journey that requires God's supernatural counsel and sometimes the help of a great therapist. However, if you are willing to stick with it, you will see God repair the breach. He takes what has been broken and fully restores what has been lost (Isaiah 58:12).

When a breach occurs, it's common to feel alone. The ones that cause the most pain are often closest to our hearts and hard to share with others. When we feel broken in the healing process, we can find relief knowing God has promised to restore us. Believe me, He knows you are hurting and will never leave you in your trial (Jer 30:17).

To "Go Get Your Life" means to live the life divinely designed for us filled with all we desire and deserve. Unforgiveness interferes with our opportunity to live our best life and is medically proven to increase sickness and disease. Our bodies were never designed to hold on to hurt.

The path of forgiveness is incredibly rewarding. According to an article released by The John Hopkins Hospital, the act of forgiveness offers enormous benefits for our health. Forgiveness lowers the risk of heart attack and improves cholesterol levels and sleep. Forgiveness also reduces pain and lowers blood pressure.

There are also psychological rewards to forgiveness. When we release the anger and resentment, we create room for empathy towards the person who has wronged us. The more forgiving we are, the more content we will be. According to Karen Swartz, M.D., director of the Mood Disorders Adult Consultation Clinic at John Hopkins Hospital, forgiveness eliminates stress, anxiety, anger, hostility, and depression.

Finally, there is a tremendous spiritual reward for forgiving—we are also forgiven. The verse "Forgive us our sins, as we have forgiven those who sin against us" demonstrates that *as* we forgive we will be forgiven (Matthew 6:12). In forgiving those we feel are undeserving, we not only find peace, but we also receive forgiveness for ourselves.

Regardless of what breach occurred, scripture reminds us that we have everything we need—in ourselves and from God—to forgive whoever has wronged us. No matter how deep or long ago the breach occurred, it can be repaired with forgiveness. The One who *is* the repairer of all things will bring you into complete and total restoration.

Definition of Breach:
An infraction or violation of a law, trust, faith, or promise.

Definition of Repairer:
A skilled worker who mends or repairs things.

Prayer Before You Act:

Dear God, thank you for the gift of forgiveness and the strength to forgive those who have harmed me. Show me how to let go of any anger, bitterness, hurt, or hostility that I may be holding on to. Free me from anything that tries to creep in through the root of unforgiveness. Help me address what I have ignored so I can be healed. Amen.

Action Step:

Are there any past breaches that overcame? How did God help you in your time of need? Take a few minutes to write down what you went through and how you experienced victory. Secondly, identify a breach you've recently been struggling with. What is one step you can take to bring healing to your breach? Remember, we need to release every breach for our own freedom, peace, and happiness!

WALK IT OUT

DAY THIRTY-FOUR

*Don't fret or worry. Instead of worrying, pray. Let petitions
and praises shape your worries into prayers, letting God
know your concerns. Before you know it, a sense of God's
wholeness, everything coming together for good,
will come and settle you down. It's wonderful what happens when
Christ displaces worry at the center of your life.*
~ Philippians 4:6-7 (MSG)

I know a young lady whose goal was to become a doctor. I had the personal pleasure of attending her college graduation, where she graduated with honors in the School of Science and Biology. From an early age, she knew she wanted to help people and understood the dedication required to make her dream come true.

Because of her achievements, she received multiple acceptance letters from several medical schools around the country. After much deliberation, she settled on her decision. It wouldn't be her first choice. However, it would be the most practical. She would attend a school near her hometown.

That would allow her to receive active support from her family through the grueling medical school process.

On the day she received her undergraduate, she was surprised to receive a notification that her dream school had accepted her. Completely shocked, she began to weigh a very tough decision. If she chose to make this last-minute decision, her housing, roommate, and financial aid would all be affected. The excitement of graduation day was quickly overshadowed by the time-sensitive decision.

Quickly, everyone in her family and friend group had an opinion. Many traveled a great distance to celebrate with her. I could tell she wanted a moment to think about the choice while simultaneously enjoying this special day with her friends and loved ones.

Later that day, guests congratulated her on her medical school plans during the graduation party. So many people were excited for her to move back to her home state. Only a few of us in the room knew that her plans were still in the air.

During the party, I could sense how uncomfortable she was while she tried to enjoy the celebration. Her family toasted to a future that might not exist. The cake matched the medical school she was no longer sure she would be attending. As I left the party, I reminded her not to worry because God would be with her no matter the decision she made. Yes, she may have to disappoint some people and deal with some financial repercussions. I encouraged her to make this decision with God's prompting and leading and without the opinions of man (Psalm 146:3). I told her that this would be something she would need to walk out and find peace. That made me think of a toddler learning to walk.

I told her that even if she were to stumble or fall while making this decision, she would not have to take these steps alone. God would be holding His arms out to support her like our parents did when we first began to walk (Philippians 3:12-14). I knew that she would make the best decision if she trusted God. She would not get stuck if she continued to move forward and ask Him for guidance.

When a young child takes their first steps, their parents encourage them to take them by faith. They say things like "you can do it!" or "come on, get up!" to push children forward. Parents know their children will learn to walk if they don't give up. This process is much like the steps we take toward any life challenge. With God we can trust that the outcome is good.

We must learn to trust God so that no matter what. We can walk towards our choices and trust in His guidance. Even when we stumble and fall, we must get up and keep moving forward. Instead of worrying about our path, we should pray for God to lead, guide, and support us until we receive what He has promised us (Philippians 4:6-7).

In the weeks that followed my friend's graduation night, confirmations followed every faithful step. The school that initially accepted her in her hometown did not penalize her for the withdrawals. She found someone to take over her lease for her original apartment. She also transitioned seamlessly to her new program. It was evident she had made the right choice. The key was to keep walking it out by faith for the things she wanted. God was faithful (Philippians 4:6).

God wants you to experience His very best. He wants to be involved in your decisions and guide you along your path (Ephesians 1:11). He wants you to put your trust in Him and refuse to worry. This way you can go get the life He has called you to live. Today, trust in the Lord, and He will direct your path.

Definition of Walk:

Move at a regular pace by lifting and setting down each foot in turn. Guide, accompany, or escort someone on foot.

Prayer Before You Act:

Dear God, Thank you for moving me forward with your divine direction today and every day of my life. I trust you to protect me if I stumble and fall. You know the challenges I face and the direction I should go. As I acknowledge you in all my ways, help me submit to your will for my life. Provide me with confirmation, so I hear your voice and follow your direction. Amen.

Action Step:

Is there any unfinished business in your life? It can be as small as cleaning your room or as big as returning to school. Write down how different your life would be and how different you would feel if you could accomplish it. Are there any simple steps you can take right now to get closer to completion?

OVERNIGHT BAG

DAY THIRTY-FIVE

*For, "The One who wants to enjoy life and see good days
[good—whether apparent or not] must keep his tongue free from
evil and his lips from speaking guile (treachery, deceit).*
~ 1 Peter 3:10

To deceive means to cause someone to believe something that is not true, typically for a personal advantage. The enemy specializes in tricking us. He accomplishes this by luring us off track with distractions. Sometimes, the enemy can even use us to derail people off their purpose paths. Other times, he uses our weaknesses to deceive ourselves.

I've had to work diligently to avoid self-deception over the years. As a result, I have been able to help many others break out of those patterns as well. To this day, I purposefully think through my daily decisions. If there is a decision I'm unsure of, I will pray about it and sleep on it until I receive inner peace. Making good choices requires sound wisdom and logical reasoning.

One time when my children were much younger, I went on a writing retreat. As I packed my overnight bag, tears welled up in my eyes. I knew the underlying reason for my abrupt exit was not quite right. While it was true that I had missed multiple publishing deadlines and needed a place to focus, I also was feeling sorry for myself. I had not given my husband and kids the opportunity to support me in my writing journey. I was running away.

I had deceived myself into thinking they didn't understand the pressure I was under. I justified my decision to flee by telling myself that this trip would be best for everyone.

As I wept, I saw my children peeking through the bedroom door. They had come to see what all the noise was about. When they noticed I spotted them, they ran away giggling, which brought me some peace. Soon I heard them talking to their father in his office, which, even as adults, is a place they still receive counsel.

They asked, "Why is mommy leaving? Is she mad at us?"

As I reflected, it became evident that I had allowed the enemy to deceive me. In reality, I had all the support I needed. This was a me vs. me situation. It was true that I was stressed about an overdue writing assignment. Still, my fear of rejection had opened the door to deception.

As I sat on the edge of the bed, my tears of frustration turned into weeping. I did not want writing success if it caused me to behave in this way. I had to be honest with myself and accept the truth.

John 16:13 says, "When the Spirit of truth comes, he will guide you into all the truth, for he will not speak on his own authority, but whatever he hears he will speak, and he will declare to you the things that are to come." When we choose to speak the truth, we cast away deception. To quote Cornel West, "There is a price to pay for speaking the truth. There is a bigger price for living a lie."

Even if you initially suffer for being honest, you're still better off than being deceived. Resist the lies of the enemy. Through thick and thin, keep your hearts listening to Christ, your Master. Be ready to speak up even if what you know to be true is hard to accept. Keep a clear conscience before God so that you can resist the lies of the enemy.

The most powerful lies come from within. I have to resist believing lies in my head daily. Let's pay close attention to the enemy's deception. It's time to renew our minds with God's transformational assistance.

Definition of Deceive:

To cause someone to believe something that is not true, typically to gain some personal advantage. To give a mistaken impression or fail to admit to oneself that something is true.

Prayer Before You Act:

Lord, as I spend time with You in your presence, reveal to me those areas that I have been deceived. Help me resist the lies of the enemy and speak Your truths over my life. Amen.

Action Step:

What lie about yourself have you entertained? Flip the statement into a truth you want to see manifested. Write this declaration in your journal to remind yourself of the power of speaking truth. Be confident that the words you speak are backed by God's power to deliver the results you seek, speak, and expect!

Example: Turn an Untrue Thought into a Truth Statement

Untrue Thought: "No one supports me."

Truth Statement: "I have all the help and support I need to achieve everything I am called to do!"

SMOOTH LIKE BUTTER

DAY THIRTY-SIX

But now, O Lord, you are our father;
we are the clay, and you are our potter;
we are all the work of your hand.
~ Isaiah 64:8 ESV

My father's macaroni and cheese—a recipe he learned from a cook in the Detroit Lions cafeteria—has been a family favorite for years. It was a staple dish at the table for every holiday and special occasion. On the first Christmas without my dad, no one attempted to cook a knock-off version. Unlike boxed mac and cheese, my father used several kinds of cheese, heavy cream, barrels of butter, elbow macaroni, and secret spices. A golden crust of burnt cheese and butter around the outer rim of the pan sizzled and cracked when it was taken out of the oven.

I knew that if I was going to recreate my father's beloved dish, I had to nail the outer crust. Not knowing exactly how he pulled it off, I began to google different recipes. Kettle cooked mac and cheese could produce the crunchy, cheesy, and crusty effect by creating a soft butter lining.

The first time I decided to attempt to make this complex recipe was an hour before guests arrived on Thanksgiving. At that time, the only available butter was still in the freezer and solid as a rock. Knowing the microwave would melt the butter inconsistently, I decided to warm them by holding the container in my hands.

The plan worked until I noticed the center was frozen. My solution was to cut the sticks and soften the smaller pieces by moving them around in my hand. The longer I held the butter pads, the more pliable they became.

As I molded the butter and thought of my father, I thought about some of the ways he shaped his children. When we were young, he often used tough love, long lectures, and spankings to teach us how to behave (Proverbs 13:24). When we were teenagers, he dropped wisdom nuggets frequently. Once we were adults, my father still would randomly call us and request to meet one-on-one. Even though those meetings were often intense, you made sure to show up on time.

While I continued to heat up the butter in my hand, I started to think about how God shapes us. His ways are the best because He knows us better than we know ourselves (Romans 8:27). Even if we didn't have the best molders or shapers raising us, God has made provision for that as well (Psalm 27:10).

In the same way that butter is molded with heat, we are also molded through friction. The heat we experience through pressure, challenge, and trouble often prepares us to overcome. In those hard times, we often become willing, motivated, and humble enough for God to shape us. When we put our struggles in God's hands, His spirit will soften and reshape past hurts, failures, and disappointments.

Transformation at the hand of God can be uncomfortable sometimes, but it is essential to personal development. Like a potter who centers clay on a wheel, God will keep you centered if you put yourself in His hands (Psalm 31:15). He is shaping you to make you better. The outcome will be beauty. He does not disappoint (Psalm 25:2).

Definition of a Potter's Wheel:

A machine used in the shaping (known as throwing) of round ceramic ware known as clay. The wheel may also be used while trimming the excess body from leather hard-dried ware (stiff but malleable) and for applying incised decoration or rings of color.

Prayer Before You Act:

Dear Heavenly Father, I surrender my unfavorable circumstances to you today and release any resentment towards others who may have had a hand in creating them. I also forgive myself for contributing to those circumstances. Give me the patience to heal. I place my challenges before you and pray for the discipline to stay on the "wheel" while you mold me to become better and better. You are the potter, and I am the clay. Amen!

Action step:

Take a few minutes and spend time with God today. Ask him to reveal the things in your heart that need the molding of the Holy Spirit and ask Him to heal and restore.

PREPARE FOR TAKE OFF

DAY THIRTY-SEVEN

Now I will relieve your shoulder of its burden;
I will free your hands from their heavy tasks.
~ Psalm 81:6 (TLB)

Taking off means to take flight and become airborne like a bird. Other meanings include to leave, bolt, flee, go, depart, or escape.

There was a time I traveled so much that I lived out of a suitcase. When I had time to wash my clothes, I was already repacking them for another trip. Public speaking invitations were increasing along with high-profile coaching clients across the country. I wanted to capitalize on my growing opportunities and improve my gift of helping people connect with their God-given purpose. I knew that meant I had to sacrifice time away with my family.

I found myself walking the jet-way frequently with every passing month. That meant more prayers for safe flights. My travel ritual included touching the top and both sides of the hatch before entering the plane and whispering a quick prayer. Once inside, I turned to the cockpit and quickly stretched my hand out to bless the pilots, flight instruments, and crew before taking my seat. Even if I caught a few stares from the other passengers, I didn't care. In fact, I primarily received thankful smiles and nods.

Then one early morning, after taking my seat, something unexpected happened. After flight instructions and cabin check, I heard the intercom announce, "Prepare for take-off!" I had just sat down with enough time to buckle my belt and push my purse under the seat. I wondered how it was already time to take off. Again, I heard, "Prepare for take-off." Suddenly, I realized it was the audible voice of the Spirit of God whispering to me and not the captain flying the plane.

I focused so I could better hear God's voice inside of me. It said, "When you get ready to fly, there are several instructions for a safe take-off, flight, and landing. If you avoid any of these steps, unfavorable outcomes might occur. These include plane removal, delayed departures, or a crash landing."

I began to ponder what God was trying to tell me. Before you fly successfully, there are many protocols you must follow: I.D. checks, bag weight, security checks, seat belt regulations, smoking laws, and liquid restrictions. Why was God speaking to me through airport terminology?

A flight can also be delayed or canceled due to factors outside the plane, like weather or scheduling conflicts. If the wings become icy, their ability to take-off and keep the plane airborne is drastically reduced. The plane can be too heavy, or its cargo can be improperly balanced.

The more I reflected, the more I understood the meaning of "prepare for take-off." Finally, it clicked. "Am I really ready for what He promised to still do in my life?" I asked myself. "Am I ready to go where I have asked God to take me? Am I really ready to land into the next stage of my life?"

I realized that I needed to jettison unnecessary weights if I wanted to soar through the next season of my life. It was time to let go of some things that prevented me from reaching my destination. There were things I might be able to check for a later pickup, but some had to be removed at security. Asking someone else to hold the extra bags was not an option.

During ascension, the atmospheric changes create turbulence when passing through air pockets. Ears may pop from pressure changes, and your stomach might turn. Often passengers close their eyes tightly or clench the hand of their travel companion.

Everyone in the aircraft feels the tangible shift taking place in and around the plane. This is much like the changes that occur in and around us as we navigate through life. It can be scary and uncomfortable. You may have to grab support from someone close to you when you feel like things are spinning. There are bumps and moments of stillness as you ascend.

God's gentle whisper to "prepare for takeoff" has stuck with me and helped me understand why we don't have to worry. There is peace when we release our burdens to God (1 Peter 5:7). They are not always our own. We have to recognize what others asked us to carry and those that we inherited. Many burdens are seasonal and should only be held for short periods of time.

There are some things God has given us the grace to carry, but there are others that only hinder our ascension (Matthew 11:30). The enemy can deceive us into holding onto things and people out of obligation (2 Corinthians 2:11). We should first be obligated to fulfill our calling. You have God's divine permission to unapologetically pursue your dreams (Ephesians 2:10)!

To walk purposely requires several round trips along the way. Remember, with each season in life, there are new assignments (Luke 12:48). You can expect pockets of turbulence, unpredictable storms, and delays as you ascend. There will be landing points to catch your breath and layovers for rest in between. The Lord wants you to surrender your burdens to Him so that you will always have successful take-offs and smooth landings. Eventually, unnecessary baggage will become an issue as you go higher and further into your calling.

Prepare for take-off in every way by removing unnecessary baggage, carrying only what is only necessary, buckling up during rocky moments, and remaining planted in your assigned position. You must trust the instructions from the captain of your life, God. Step by step and leg to leg through the journey, stay tuned to His voice through daily prayer and meditation. I guarantee He will speak to you through promptings and confirming signs. He most likely won't speak to you through an airplane intercom, but He will speak to your inner man. You are taking the flight of your life, and God is the captain. Buckle up! You are in for the adventure of a lifetime!

Definition of Baggage:
Past experiences or long-held ideas regarded as burdens and impediments.

Definition of Check:
An examination to test or ascertain the accuracy, quality, or satisfactory condition.

Prayer Before You Act:
Dear God, help me to hear your instructions for my life. Show me what I must let go of so that I might inherit your Kingdom and glory. Empower me to release unnecessary baggage. I know you will lead, guide, and carry me through the amazing life you have called me to life. Be with me at every stop so I may answer my divine assignments.

Action Step:
Take a moment to identify the baggage in your personal life, and write out the issue and/or the person(s) attached to it. Choose up to three of these "bags" and write down the root cause of why you hold them. Once you have done so, find three solutions to releasing all of them!

LOBSTER MASHED POTATOES

DAY THIRTY-EIGHT

But if we look forward to something we don't yet have,
we must wait patiently and confidently.
~ Romans 8:25 (NLT)

I consider myself a foodie. I love beautiful presentations of food anywhere as long as they're delicious. However, considering my diet, former struggles with obesity, and my life coaching, I have to manage my indulgence. I have to remain vigilant in order to keep from binging, which was the main cause of weighing 328 pounds at one point in my life. I learned that by allowing myself a weekly cheat meal would motivate me to eat clean and resist temptation.

One day, while watching the food network, I saw a dish that captured my curiosity. It may be a popular dish now but at the time only two fine dining restaurants within driving distance offered lobster mashed potatoes. Luckily, Mother's Day was approaching, so I seized the opportunity to choose our dinner location and taste this dish for the first time.

Upon arrival, I waited with great anticipation and soaked up the restaurant's ambiance. I paced myself by eating small portions of the truffle popcorn and freshly baked sourdough bread.

Throughout the dinner, I raved about the photos and reviews for the lobster mashed potatoes. When they arrived, I was severely disappointed. The lobster mashed potatoes were housed in a beautiful sterling silver bowl with cold, decorative handles. There was not a smidgen of steam in sight when I scooped them onto my plate. I was not about to let my weekly cheat meal go to waste! The waiter insisted on having new ones made rather than warming the ones on my plate. I didn't care how he went about it as long as they were brought back hot before I finished my steak.

After a while, he returned and apologetically set the new dish on the table. From my seat, I could see the potatoes looked much different than the last order. They had a strange, runny texture. I asked the waiter to stand by while I scooped a portion onto my plate. As I suspected, they ran straight through the slats. I was baffled. Why would this establishment send them to the table like this in the first place?

I was losing my desire for the dish I had waited for weeks to eat. I'm sure my reaction made the table feel a bit uncomfortable. They would rather I just pay for the cold, runny potatoes than to say another word about it. Despite the embarrassment of my children, I sent the dish back a second time.

I was certain the restaurant expected us to pay at least $28 for a side of lobster mashed potatoes. There was even a dress code required to sit at the white linen-covered tables. I thought I would receive a five-star dining experience for an expensive price. This was hardly the case. I was willing to send them back until they were made properly on my cheat day.

Since I wasn't eating, I capitalized on a teaching moment. While they made the potatoes a third time, I asked our children to compare their lives to the expectations for this dinner. Then I asked what they felt was expected from them to receive whatever it was they were expecting.

We can't send our lives back to the kitchen for a do-over. We also can't put them in the microwave to heat them up quickly. Regardless, we shouldn't accept a watered-down life either.

Because God sent Jesus, we have an opportunity for an abundant life in this fallen world (John 10:10). This type of abundance refers to a life full of joy and strength for the spirit, soul, and body. Knowing that we have access to live out the abundant life should motivate us never to settle.

God wants us to expect the very best life that heavenly Father has ordered for us. He has made plans that are far beyond the scope of what we can ask, think, or imagine. No matter who you are or where you are in life, there are always challenges to overcome. We should desire nothing less than to pursue it. Like I persisted in getting my order right, we should be relentless in pursuing the dreams God has given us. Yes, there are mistakes, mishaps, and misdirections, but if we aim our expectations high and believe in God, we can experience all that He has for us (1 Samuel 12:16).

I knew how great those potatoes should have tasted, but my family had no baseline to gauge the result. They did not understand my potato passion. My children didn't regularly experience this level of food service that I frequented with their Dad. But I, on the other hand, would accept nothing less than what I came for: award-winning lobster mashed potatoes as seen on TV.

Know the difference between God's expectations of you and the expectations of others (Romans 4:20-21). We don't want the wrong things in our lives, even if they're presented nicely like those lobster mashed potatoes were. This is why it is so important to spend time in God's presence and inquire about His plan. He gives us the clearest picture of what we want so that we can reject the wrong opportunities. We must learn to be bold when it comes to pursuing the life God intended for us.

Thankfully, God won't mess up our lives and serve cold, runny plans. In fact, His plans are solid because they were created before the foundation of the Earth. Expect God's best, don't accept any mess, and ORDER UP!

Definition of Order:

Give an authoritative direction or instruction to do something. Request (something) to be made, supplied, or served.

Prayer Before You Act:

Lord, help me to be patient as I wait for your promises to be fulfilled. Please reveal what this looks like so I will know what to accept and what to reject. You have called me growth in every area of my life no matter where I am today. Help me to receive it. Amen.

Action Step:

Was there a time when you settled for less than what you knew God had for you? Maybe it was in a relationship, a job, or financially. Take five minutes and write yourself a reminder for your future self to pursue God's best. ,Remember this rule the next time you have an opportunity to reject something that does not align with God's best!

IT'S BETTER TOGETHER

DAY THIRTY-NINE

Two are better than one because they have a good reward for their toil.
For if they fall, one will lift up his fellow. But woe to him who
is alone when he falls and has not another to lift him up!
~ Ecclesiastes 4:9-10 (ESV)

Being one of the oldest siblings in a large family, I often had to figure some things out alone. I began to believe that flying solo minimized the opportunity to be disappointed. To my detriment, I carried that belief into my early years in business. Thinking I had to do everything alone, I lost a lot of time learning the value of delegation, partnership, and trust.

During that initial learning curve, I almost lost my business, which would have ruined the livelihoods of several people. Eventually, I had to take on a partner for the first time ever. It was a humbling experience that caused me to mature as a businesswoman and as a person. I had done all I could alone and realized that two really were better than one. I had always been leery of someone hijacking my vision or making suggestions I disagreed with. Thankfully, my new partner really understood the "co" in cooperate, and I haven't had to revisit that lesson for nearly 30 years!

Ecclesiastes 4 explains the value of partnership. Solomon reflects on the importance of companionship and the value of working together in this passage. He reminds us of the stress that accompanies "going at it alone." He reiterates that no matter how overwhelmed we get, we must have people who help us get back up and on track.

There are endless ways to become socially, spiritually, and emotionally isolated. Partnership—with a doctor, coach, trainer, or pastor—will help us find our way out.

As human beings, we are social creatures. We need one another for encouragement, sharpening, and correction to become our best (Proverbs 27:17). We can see supernatural increase in our lives when we partner with God and improve our relationship with him (1 Corinthians 3:6-8).

There will be those we encounter who plant seeds of encouragement. Others will water those seeds. We will only go so far without adding God to this equation. God brings the increase and the promotions to our lives (Psalm 75:6-7)!

At the beginning of today's devotional, we learned the benefits of partnerships and the detriments of going at it alone. You are never alone even while waiting for Him to surround you with the right partners (Joshua 1:9). He is your ultimate partner and perfect supporter. He goes before you and follows behind you. I cannot think of a better partner to do life with (Isaiah 52:12).

Definition of Cooperation:

The process of working together to the same end. Assistance, especially by ready compliance with requests.

Prayer Before You Act:

God, thank you for being the president of my fan club and my biggest supporter. Surround me with the right partners so that I might fulfill the plans you have set before me. Direct my path and place people on it who are assigned to assist me with my purpose. Help me to know how long these partnerships should last and protect me from anything that would cause hindrances to my progress. Thank you for being my trusted guide as I journey to achieve all you have sent me to fulfill. Amen.

Action Step:

When was the last time you partnered with someone in a way that benefited you? What is an area of your life you would benefit from a partnership today? Take a few moments and ask God to surround you with the right partners at the right times.

THINK. PREPARE. COMMIT.

DAY FORTY

Good planning and hard work lead to prosperity,
but hasty shortcuts lead to poverty.
~ Proverbs 21:5 (NLT)

When our children were very young, they often asked for toys, ice cream, and to play outside. Our answer sometimes would be, "Not today, but maybe we can tomorrow!"

They would usually reply, "TO-NOW, Mommy! Not tomorrow...to-now!" They had created the clever phrase and believed that saying "to-now" would actually get them whatever they wanted! Their serious tone and the entitled looks on their cute little faces would always make me laugh.

As adults, we understand most requests take time. Even instant rice takes five minutes to cook. Instant coffee still requires water, heat, and stirring. Life is not microwavable. Often our most significant breakthroughs that seem to appear suddenly—like an overnight success—always have a lengthy backstory. The things we want the most take time to acquire. We all pay our dues in one way or another.

I had always worked hard to chase my dreams. However, there were many times I felt like I still couldn't catch them. I had the vision and the drive. Yet, something always seemed to get in the way. A roadblock, blindside, or curve-ball would inevitably show up.

I was caught in a cycle of unproductiveness. My time was monopolized by business emergencies and other people's problems. I needed more time to perform tasks that would move my dreams forward. By believing the fallacy that I could "do it all," I sacrificed precious time meant for achieving specific goals.

After I turned thirty, I evaluated my life's vital components. This would turn into an annual practice of reviewing my progress and carefully considering what I wanted the next 365 days to look like. I would also check my goals from the previous year and identify areas I could improve. Finally, I would write down why I did not accomplish certain things and why I was successful at others (Proverbs 4:7).

This annual check in would not only allow me to identify bad habits that I needed to change but also ways to increase my productivity. It allowed me to clearly articulate my vision for the coming year.

At first, I struggled to keep the vow I had made. The busy holiday season made it hard to think, reflect, and plan. It pushed me to strategically utilize the twenty-four hours of each day (Ephesians 5:15). I needed to learn how to divide my time efficiently and adequately manage my faith, family, finance, fitness, friends, and fun (Colossians 4:5).

Over time, I improved. Eventually, I would call this process "F-ing" my life up. Before you let your mind wander too far, there are at least 10,141 words in the English dictionary beginning with the letter F, including those six listed in my mantra: "Elevate and escalate your faith, family, finance, fitness, friends, and fun to live the life you desire and deserve."

By elevating and escalating those six vital components of life each year, you will live *through purpose, on purpose, and in your purpose.*

God never intended for you to move through your day like on a hamster wheel (Deuteronomy 2:3). He designed you to live an abundant life full of purpose. However, we have to position ourselves to receive it.

Unfortunately, a thief is roaming the Earth whose only mission is to kill, steal, and destroy your life by robbing you of your time, talent, and treasure (John 10:10). Therefore, you must remain vigilant in preventing his plans. You can do that by intentionally pursuing what God wants for you.

Your life evaluation is just as important as your annual doctor's appointment. Look at each year as the pre-launch before the official release of a product. In marketing, a pre-launch is meant to raise awareness and build excitement. We should do the same when headed into new times, seasons, and endeavors for our lives. Each new year is one of them.

The term "New Year's Resolution" is often misused because resolutions usually don't create lasting change. About 60% of people don't make one, and of those that do, only 7% keep their promises for the new year. It took me a while to become a part of the 7%. It was only possible through dedication, discipline, and much of God's grace.

Let this year be the year you stop the cycle of busy unproductiveness. Instead of following Nike's mantra of "Just Do It," make the decision today to "Just Pursue It!" Pursue God's will for your faith, family, finance, fitness, friends, and fun. That means taking three simple steps: think, prepare, and commit. Watch what God will do.

Definition of Pursue:

To follow, overtake, capture, kill, or defeat. To find or employ measures to obtain or accomplish: seek or pursue a goal.

Prayer Before You Act:

Dear God, reveal the areas in my life that need to be elevated and escalated this season. Help me use my time correctly to produce the results I want. Teach me the strategies to fulfill your purpose and desire for my life. Order my steps and illuminate my path. With your help, I can scale any wall on my way to victory (Psalm 18). Amen.

Action Step:

1. THINK about two goals that fall within faith, family, finance, fitness, food, or fun you are closest to achieving.

2. PREPARE a strategy that fits your current lifestyle to achieve that goal.

3. COMMIT to applying your approach daily until your goals are fulfilled.

Acknowledgments

My father often reminded me, "You think you have more time than you do...but you don't." That phrase kept pushing me through to finish this long-awaited and anticipated devotional. I knew it would benefit the reader and stir them to fulfill their earthly assignments. I also knew that finishing *Go Get Your Life!* after years of preparation and contemplation would be one of the biggest assignments I'd ever need to complete!

I thank God for giving me the pen of a ready writer. It has allowed me to share what I believe to be a life-changing book for millions who want to live life to the fullest.

I cannot thank my family, friends, and team enough for working patiently with me to labor and deliver *Go Get Your Life!* I would like to thank my husband, Marcus, for always holding everything down and lifting me up. To my daughter Maranda and my two sons Marcus and Christian, who loved, encouraged, and held me accountable throughout this two-year process. To my mother, Georgianna, thank you for reminding me, even as a child, that we can do anything we set our minds to if we just believe. The mantra "You can do it, you can do it, if you put your mind to it!" still motivates me today. To my late father Charles, whose work ethic and tenacity taught me so much. Your mantle will always rest upon me. I pray you and Mom Juanita Sailor are smiling down as witnesses from the clouds.

Thank you to my amazing sister Georgie, an armor bearer who always has my back. You are my true friend! By His hand, you have helped me through tough seasons and challenging days that most people will never see.

A special thank you to my father-in-law Calvin "Popeye" Sailor, who sowed into my vision at the "midnight hour" and stands by in support of anything I need at any time. I'm forever grateful to Tim Storey—my Pastor, life coach, brother, friend, and fellow World-shaker—for always believing in me. You told me I would write several books over 20 years ago! Your mentorship and willingness to connect me to your friends and colleagues have changed my life and this project! One was Paul Lambert, who took the time to serve me while producing his major play. Your enthusiasm to empower me to reach the next stage of my life has meant the world to me. Paul, we are going into a new orbit.

I am also immensely grateful to Stefan and Calandra Junaeus and the entire Signature Message publishing team. You have hearts of gold which may be why you have the Midas touch! Everything you touch turns to gold. Stefan, your knowledge and expertise in publishing, your unique processes, and your peaceful demeanor helped this milestone to manifest. "Callie," I appreciate your genuine concern for me and this special project while assisting me in the social media and branding space. You definitely have the patience to match my urgency. That's a true gift!

Special thanks to Christian Ophus at Emerge Publishing for designing this amazing book cover and coaching me in ways I never knew I needed as an author, coach, and public speaker. You are a general in the world of publishing!

And to Derrick Boucher at Salt Sound Marketing for your constant support through every shift and change of my digital presence. Your precision and patience are valuable assets that I'm so grateful to have had the opportunity to experience.

To all of my "sister-friends" and my prayer group, "Table of Five," who have covered and encouraged me daily…I love you, and thank God you still love me through it all.

Thank you to the "Go Get Your Life with Coach Charese" Facebook group members and followers of the "Gather, Grow, and Glow!" empowerment meetings. Your love and support have been heartfelt. Being able to minister to you as I wrote this book has also ministered to me and made a difference on this journey.

To The Beauty Studios, Inc. family of suite salons. Thank you for releasing me to become an author while trusting me to keep the businesses flowing and going as an overseer and entrepreneur.

Thank you for every form of support that made it possible to convey my vision of helping others live the lives they desire and deserve!

I dedicate *Go Get Your Life!* to you and declare that you will do just that!

Free Clarity Coaching Session from Coach Charese

Now you can get clear on your goals, purpose and direction...

If you are ready to:

- Take responsibility for the dreams that belong to you!
- Be intentional towards becoming the best you can be!
- Willing to remove old mindsets and trust new processes!
- Become excited about your future & willing to fight for it!

Then receive the gift of a
Free Clarity Coaching Session
from Coach Charese by visiting:

www.GoGetYourLifeBook.com/clarity

Use this QR code with your cel phone for immediate access:

Find more tools to help you Go Get Your Life!
at *www.GoGetYourLifeBook.com*

Made in the USA
Columbia, SC
10 February 2023

11852260R00091